FACING TODAY

FACING
TODAY

VOLUME 1

Text copyright © BRF 1993

Published by
The Bible Reading Fellowship
Peter's Way
Sandy Lane West
Oxford
OX4 5HG
ISBN 0 7459 2589 8
Albatross Books Pty Ltd
PO Box 320, Sutherland
NSW 2232, Australia
ISBN 0 7324 0766 4

First edition 1993

Acknowledgments

Scriptures quoted from the Good News Bible published by The Bible Societies/HarperCollins Publishers Ltd., UK © American Bible Society, 1966, 1971, 1976, 1992, with permission.

The Holy Bible, New International Version, copyright © 1973, 1978, 1984 by International Bible Society. Used by permission of Hodder and Stoughton Limited.

The Revised Standard Version of the Bible, copyright © 1946, 1952, 1971 by the Division of Christian Education of the National Council of the Churches of Christ in the USA.

The New Revised Standard Version of the Bible, copyright © 1989 by the Division of Christian Education of the National Council of the Churches of Christ in the USA.

A catalogue record for this book is available from the British Library

Printed and bound in Malta

Contents

Introduction

This book is an excellent resource for anyone who has anything to do with groups in churches. The BRF used to resource churches in this area of their life through the old 'S' notes—'S' standing for study. We are still getting requests for them, but many are now out of date or have run out. This book is our solution to the problem—and is volume 1 of a series which we shall produce each year.

Here is a selection of five courses which deal with five different areas of importance to church life. They cover: various issues for today; spirituality and Christian maturity; Christian stewardship; the letter to the Philippians; and a confirmation course for young people. You can choose whichever course you wish to use. Once you have done so you can (with the exception of 'Faithful Stewards') obtain further copies of that particular course in packs of ten either from your local bookshop or direct from BRF. Thus each member of your group can have their own copy.

The course 'Issues for Today' was produced in the Diocese of Oxford to enable church groups to consider the really pressing issues of the day in the context of the Bible. The facilitators wanted to do this in a way that would be helpful for any sort of group: for people who are not particularly learned or who are learned; for people with a lot of time to give to the study or only a little; and also for people whose children might be running around whilst the group was in progress. Penny Nairne is a Reader and is involved in adult lay training in the Diocese of Oxford. At the moment she is particularly interested in exploring imaginative methods of reading the Bible in groups and through participative Bible study.

'Spirituality and Christian Maturity' was produced for St Mary's Church in Reigate, Surrey, in response to the hunger which many people were expressing for the deeper things of God, and for a spirituality which quenched the thirst of the soul as well as an instruction and study that fed the mind. I wrote the introduction and three of the studies, and Jean Francis wrote the other three. She is a geographer who has been head of three secondary modern schools. She has a deep interest in spirituality, and loves long country walks and cooking meals for her friends.

'Faithful Stewards' was used in Oxshott, Surrey, in 1991 at a stewardship renewal campaign. There had been several campaigns before, and after this one the whole parish seemed to take on a new lease of life and gained a new perspective on Christian stewardship. They set up a range of study groups, for a range of abilities, and these were enjoyed by all involved. If you are to use this course in your parish everyone will need a copy of the book, since there are Bible readings and reflections for six weeks which look at every aspect of Christian stewardship and therefore, inevitably, at the whole of the Christian life. Each week culminates in a group meeting, for which material is provided plus leaders' notes. Averil Bamber is a Reader in the Church of England and says that her interests are theology and gardening.

'The Letter to the Philippians' has been one of the most popular S[tudy] notes over the years, and since it is no longer available in that form it is reprinted here.

'Walking in the Light' is an eight-week confirmation course for young people. Tim Mayfield produced it for his parish in Halifax, Yorkshire, and it works very effectively. He has written leaders' notes for each week to show you just how it can be used.

We are most grateful to Sarah Finch, of Friends of the Earth, for all her helpfulness (and speed) in checking out and bringing up to date our figures and statistics connected with the environment and with families.

Shelagh Brown
Commissioning Editor

Issues for Today

INTRODUCTION

These meetings are designed to last one hour and fifteen minutes. There is no need to have a leader in the sense of an expert, but someone will need to be responsible for time-keeping. S/he would ensure that all the material is worked through, moving the discussion smoothly through the different parts and using the suggested timings as a guide. This will mean that people are neither kept too long nor put into the position of having to leave before the end.

At the first meeting, if people do not know each other, make sure that everyone at least exchanges names and where they come from. Everyone will need to have a copy of the course and to understand the purpose of coming together. At later meetings you may wish to begin with a short recall of the last meeting to put newcomers in the picture and to keep a sense of the whole programme. People may wish to share how they are finding the sessions. This is valuable for building trust and for making any necessary changes. You may wish to share how you have taken forward your concerns since you last met. These are all ways of enriching this course. You will need to negotiate an extra fifteen minutes with the group if you decide to do anything more than the briefest recall. Be clear with the group about when this sharing has ended so that justice can be done to the new topic.

People may like to reflect on the notes for the next meeting beforehand.

Sometimes a bit of simple equipment is recommended to make the most of the session. Make sure that this is ready and to hand.

Resource people:

If you wish to take forward the issues raised in this course . . .

Your local Diocesan Board for Social Responsibility works on many of these issues, either through its own groups or through local and national ecumenical organizations.

For example, there are probably local groups of the National Churches Housing Coalition, and a Family Life and Marriage Education group which organizes courses on parenting.

In pastures green

THE ENVIRONMENT

You will need a candle and matches.

Starting where we are   *15 minutes*

Go through the following list and put a tick by each action that at least one member of the group is taking:

Conserving trees by:

☐ buying recycled paper

☐ recycling newspapers

☐ buying fewer newspapers

☐ planting a tree

☐ avoiding buying products made of hardwoods

☐ eating less beef (trees are cut to make cattle ranches).

Conserving the earth by:

☐ reusing plastic bags, preferably biodegradable ones

☐ avoiding unnecessary wrapping

☐ taking glass to a bottle bank

☐ taking aluminium cans for recycling

☐ buying organic vegetables (if you can afford them)

☐ making a compost heap.

Conserving the air and sky by:

☐ using lead-free petrol

☐ using a car with a catalytic converter

☐ avoiding aerosol sprays.

Conserving fossil fuels by:

☐ using a bicycle or going by train or walking

☐ using a fuel-efficient car

☐ using energy-efficient light bulbs

☐ cutting down on electricity consumption

☐ insulating the house

☐ fitting solar panels

Taking other action by:

☐ joining a campaign

☐ writing letters

☐ Other . . .

Looking at the wider situation

Each of the following boxes describes a situation of great concern to us all.

Working first on your own and then with a neighbour to compare your responses, draw arrows between the boxes to show how they relate to one another through cause and effect.

GLOBAL WARMING

Pollutant gases act like a greenhouse, trapping heat in the atmosphere. Rising temperatures will cause the oceans to warm and expand, leading to devastating flooding of coastal areas.

Rainfall patterns could be disrupted, causing droughts and massive crop failures.

NUCLEAR ENERGY

As Chernobyl demonstrated, there are very great risks attached to the use of nuclear power plants. Recent research has shown that nuclear power is one of the most expensive options for reducing carbon dioxide emissions.

OVER-CONSUMPTION IN RICH COUNTRIES

Although the rich countries have 24 per cent (less than a quarter) of the world's population, they consume over 80 per cent of the world's metals, chemicals and paper, 48 per cent of the world's cereals, 72 per cent of the world's milk and 64 per cent of the world's meat.

WASTE

The average household throws away one tonne of waste each year. The latest official figures ('Waste Management', Paper 28, Department of the Environment, 1991) say that the proportions of UK dustbin waste that are recyclable are as follows:

paper	60%
plastic film	60%
plastic articles	70%
textiles	50%
glass	90%
ferrous metal	80%
aluminium foil/cans	70%

There is no official figure available for how much organic waste can be composted, but it is estimated to be well over 30 per cent.

We throw away 460 million tonnes of waste every year in England and Wales from our shops, offices, factories, farms, building sites, mines and quarries. That doesn't include the millions of tonnes of liquid industrial waste and sewage effluent pumped into our rivers and seas. We also import over 40,000 tonnes of hazardous waste every year from countries which prefer not to deal with it themselves.

DESTRUCTION OF TRIBAL PEOPLES

People who have lived in the forest for thousands of years as a part of the ecosystem are being rapidly eliminated. Without their forest homes, these people rapidly die.

DEFORESTATION

It took millions of years to create tropical rain forests, but only forty years to destroy half of them. An area of tropical rain forest the size of England and Wales is lost each year—or more than one acre each second.

TWO-THIRDS WORLD DEBT

Debt repayments far exceed the financial capacity of developing countries. The desperate push for export earnings has lead to forests being felled in order to sell the timber and to convert the land into cattle ranches or plantations for export crops.

DESTRUCTION OF SPECIES

One in four medical products in our high street chemists contain compounds derived from rain-forest species. Yet every half hour a species is wiped out for ever, as rain forests are felled.

POLLUTION OF THE ATMOSPHERE

Over half of the current enhancement of the 'greenhouse effect' is caused by carbon dioxide, which is emitted by cars, industrial processes and the burning of rain forests.
Other 'greenhouse gases' are chlorofluor-ocarbons (CFCs), which remain active in the upper atmosphere for more than 100 years.

POLLUTION OF THE LAND AND WATER

More than 16 million people in Britain drink tap water which has been found to contain illegal levels of pesticides. The most acidic rain recorded in the UK fell in Scotland, and had a pH of 2.4—nearly as acidic as lemon juice. In the early 1990s more than 50 per cent of trees in western Germany were found to be seriously affected by acid rain. Over 300 million gallons of raw or virtually untreated sewage are discharged around the UK coastline every day. The UK Government allowed Britain's oil rigs and refineries to discharge 18,087 tonnes of oil in 1990.

DESERTIFICATION

Desertification is now affecting more than 100 countries. An additional 70,000 square kilometres of farmland are going out of production each year and 16,000 hectares of land are turned to desert every day.

DESTRUCTION OF OZONE LAYER

The steady build-up of chlorofluorocarbons—the gases that are used in refrigerators and in plastic foams (and were released from aerosol sprays)—and other chemicals like HCFCs, halon and methyl bromide, have been largely responsible for the destruction of the ozone layer, which protects us from the sun's ultraviolet radiation. Some 'CFC-free' aerosol sprays may contain other chemicals which destroy the ozone layer.

FUTURE

What is the future of the human race, indeed what is the future of the earth itself, if these trends continue?

Reflecting with the Bible 15 minutes

Choose one of the three sections below and work through it together.

1 Look up the first account of creation in Genesis 1. Which of the good things created by God are threatened today? How are they threatened?

2 What does God mean by giving human beings 'dominion' over creation (Genesis 1:28–30)? In Genesis 2:15 we are told that God put human beings in the garden of Eden 'to till it and keep it'. Does this help us to understand better the sort of 'dominion' we should have over the earth?

3 Look up the teaching about stewardship in Luke 12:35–48. How would you apply this parable to environmental issues? Does the idea of stewardship express the right kind of relationship between human beings and the earth?

Moving on from here *15 minutes*

Working with a neighbour, look back at the list in the 'Starting where we are' section.

Put a star by what you consider to be the most important actions to conserve the environment. Put an arrow by the ones that might be a feasible next step for you personally (even if that is something small). If you wish, and if there is time, share what you have marked with the rest of the group.

One of the best-known organizations to campaign on green issues is Friends of the Earth, 26–28 Underwood Street, London N1 7JQ. What other organizations do you know, locally or nationally, that do good work in this area? Are there any local Christian groups working for justice, peace and the integrity of creation?

Closing prayers *10 minutes*

Light a candle, then sing (or say) together:

> All creatures of our God and King,
> Lift up your voice and with us sing
> Alleluia, alleluia!
> Thou burning sun with golden beam,
> Thou silver moon with softer gleam,
> O praise him, O praise him,
> Alleluia, alleluia, alleluia!
>
> Dear mother earth, who day by day
> Unfoldest blessings on our way,
> O praise him, alleluia!
> The flowers and fruits that in thee grow,
> Let them his glory also show;
> O praise him, O praise him,
> Alleluia, alleluia, alleluia!

W.H. Draper (based on St Francis of Assisi's Canticle of the Sun)

One person then reads the following meditation:

Let us close our eyes and imagine ourselves looking in on our planet earth spinning in space, surrounded by stars and planets. (Pause)
Let us imagine ourselves coming closer and closer to the earth as it spins, and finally

landing on earth. (Pause)
We look around us and see a stream of clear, fresh water, with fish in it. (Pause)
We see the rich, dark earth. (Pause)
We see a multitude of plants and trees growing, with leaves and fruits and many
coloured flowers. (Pause)
We see animals and insects and birds happily living amongst the trees and plants. (Pause)
We breathe in the fresh, pure air. (Pause)
We give thanks and praise to God for the goodness of the world. (Pause)
We now open our eyes and say together:

God our creator, you have made us co-creators of the earth.
You have entrusted us with all the resources of the world to care for and share.
Help us always to be gentle with our planet.
Help us not to pollute the atmosphere or the waterways.
Help us not to waste precious resources like energy or food.
Help us always to be aware of the effects modern technology may have on the environment.
We ask you this through Jesus Christ our Lord. Amen.

MEETING 2

How are you?

HEALTH

You will need:

> enough magazines or colour newspaper supplements for each person to have one, plus a few extras
>
> two or three large sheets of paper and a thick felt-tipped pen
>
> a candle and matches.

One person should read through the Bible passages for the reflection in advance and decide which one should be reflected on by the group.

Starting where we are   *25 minutes*

Work on your own, tearing out of a magazine or newspaper supplement any slogans, pictures, images or shapes which say something to you about human health, about human well-being or about ill-health and disease.

> While you are doing this, it might be helpful to have in mind:
>
> the health concerns of your family and friends
>
> your own personal health concerns
>
> the health concerns of your locality
>
> the health concerns of our nation
>
> links to being a citizen of the planet.

Arrange your pieces on the floor in a collage, or just lay them out if you prefer. The point is not to make a pretty picture but in laying them out, you might find you want to make connections between them.

Then share with a neighbour why you have chosen the pieces in your collage and listen to why they have chosen theirs.

Now work together to make a list of the issues and concerns which have emerged.

Looking at the wider situation   *20 minutes*

Someone reads out:

A day scarcely goes by without one of the following topics receiving major coverage in the media: food scares, loneliness, rain forests, stress, crime rate, the Health Service, animal welfare, the ozone layer, diet ...

How do each of these topics connect to the main theme of today's topic—health? Share your ideas together and think of items in the media during the last week which might be added to this list.

'Health, wholeness and holiness are closely connected words.'

Do you agree with this statement? Test it out by looking once again at your collage and at the list which you made together. Talk about each issue or concern and see whether it fits into just one, or more than one, of the three areas: health, wholeness and holiness.

Reflecting with the Bible   *20 minutes*

Choose one of the Bible passages below. Someone reads this passage aloud, together with the notes. Everyone then talks together about the light which the passage sheds on your list, and the three areas you discussed.

Why do you keep on rebelling? Do you want to be punished even more? Israel, your head is already covered with wounds, and your heart and mind are sick. From head to foot there is not a healthy spot on your body. You are covered with bruises and sores and open wounds. Your wounds have not been cleaned or bandaged. No ointment has been put on them ... [God] says, 'Do you think I want all these sacrifices you keep offering to me? I have had more than enough of the sheep you burn as sacrifices and of the fat of your fine animals. I am tired of the blood of bulls and sheep and goats ... When you lift up your hands in prayer, I will not look at you. No matter how much you pray, I will not listen, for your hands are covered with blood. Wash yourselves clean. Stop all this evil that I see you doing. Yes, stop doing evil and learn to do right. See that justice is done—help those who are oppressed, give orphans their rights and defend widows.'

Isaiah 1:5–6, 11, 15–17 (GNB)

Notice how diseases of the body are linked with spiritual malaise and social injustice.

As Jesus was walking along, he saw a man who had been born blind. His disciples asked him, 'Teacher, whose sin caused him to be born blind? Was it his own or his parents' sin?' Jesus answered, 'His blindness has nothing to do with his sins or his parents' sins. He is blind so that God's power might be seen at work in him.'

John 9:1–3 (GNB)

Jesus rejects the crude notion that ill-health or a handicap are punishments for sin. Jesus' power over sickness and handicap is evidence of his power to forgive sin and demonstrates that his power at work in our lives is greater than that of any sin. He can release us from inner bondage which often greatly affects our physical and mental health.

[Jesus] answered John's messengers, 'Go back and tell John what you have seen and heard: the blind can see, the lame can walk, those who suffer from dreaded skin-diseases

14

are made clean, the deaf can hear, the dead are raised to life, and the Good News is preached to the poor. How happy are those who have no doubts about me!'

Luke 7:22–23 (GNB)

What are the modern equivalents of 'dreaded skin-diseases' or leprosy?

These signs of the Messiah's coming would be known to any Jew from reading the Prophets. We are meant to recognize that the peace, the *shalom* in the Hebrew, has been and is being worked out in the person and passion and resurrection of Jesus.

It is important to appreciate the rich meaning of the Hebrew word *shalom*. It is often translated as 'peace'. But if we take peace to mean just that there is no conflict or war then we might miss its much broader meaning. This broader meaning has to do with the harmony, the *true health* of creation and of society when it is informed at every level by its relationship with God.

Moving on from here   *10 minutes*

What one step can you take:
▷ in your personal life
▷ in your local setting

to make them more health-ful, that is 'full of health'.

Go on to talk together about how you might make a response in the wider scene, for example by linking with a development agency such as CAFOD or OXFAM, or by lobbying your local MP.

Closing prayers

Light a candle and make a simple pattern round it of one or two of the most important pieces of each person's collage.

Spend a few moments in silence for, as a Swedish proverb puts it, 'Silence is health.'
Bring to the silence your personal responses and resolutions from this time together.
To end, say the Lord's Prayer and the Grace together.

MEETING 3

Who cares?

COMMUNITY CARE

You will need:
a map of the local area
some paper and pencils
two large sheets of paper
a thick felt-tipped pen
a candle and matches.

Starting where we are   *20 minutes*

Using a map of the local area (Ordnance Survey will do but the bigger the scale the better), mark on it with a pin the place where you are meeting. Imagine a circle of five miles radius drawn around that pin (this area may have to be more or less than five miles depending on the density of the population around you).

Using a large sheet, work together to make a list of the caring needs that people have who live within that circle. Then go on to list everything that is already provided to care for the needs of people living there. Get some details of voluntary, family, neighbourhood, private sector and local authority provision.

Does anyone have experience of being a carer in the community? Are there any networks? Have there been any recent changes which you need to note?

From these two lists, work together to identify caring needs of this community which are very well met, and two caring needs which are very poorly met.

Looking at the wider situation   15 minutes

Different people could read out each of the paragraphs below:

In 1989, two government White Papers, 'Caring for Patients' and 'Caring for People; Community Care in the Next Decade and Beyond' tackled a restructuring of the health and care service. A new funding and planning system for community care was put into operation in 1993.

Carers, carers organizations, voluntary groups and local neighbourhood community workers are having to respond in new ways. They are building different working relationships with local authority social work agencies. They are developing a key role in monitoring provision.

They will need to continue to act as advocate. They may have to be ready to offer a bid, or a tender, to offer services where appropriate. Above all, they are ideally placed to raise the hidden issues of social injustice. They will need to work for change if it becomes evident that the gap between the quality of community care available to the rich and poor is being perpetuated or even widening.

As the plans are implemented, local authorities will be discouraged from providing services themselves but, instead, must ensure that services are provided by contracting with others, either in the private sector or the voluntary sector. The same thinking has operated in the provision of housing and education needs. We are swiftly moving towards 'welfare pluralism' with greater consumer choice. This, so the reasoning goes, will be more cost-effective and less wasteful.

Community care is about developing community alternatives to institutional provision. All political parties support this notion: Labour believes in it because it emphasizes care for the disadvantaged; the Liberal Democrats because it highlights community participation; the Conservatives because it is rooted in self-help. But community care costs money, and making that money available means making a number of complex political and economic choices.

Reflect by yourself for two minutes and choose one statement in the above paragraphs which gives you hope; and choose one statement which causes you concern.

Then talk together about your reflections.

Reflecting with the Bible   30 minutes

Take it in turns to read aloud the Bible passages and the notes that follow each section.

Do not ill-treat or oppress a foreigner; remember that you were foreigners in Egypt. Do not ill-treat any widow or orphan. If you do, I, the Lord, will answer them when they cry out to me for help, and I will be angry ...

Exodus 22:21–24 (GNB)

16

Notice that God has a special care for the vulnerable 'at risk' groups in Israel's society. Are there any links between these groups and those in your own community which you listed earlier?

The refrain 'you were foreigners in Egypt' points to the heart of Israel's hope; God in his mercy had done for Israel what she could not do for herself. When she was helpless and defenceless in Egypt, he had rescued her from her slavery there. Therefore, Israel is to treat the helpless and defenceless groups in her community as God had treated her.

When you harvest your fields, do not cut the corn at the edges of the fields, and do not go back to cut the ears of corn that were left. Do not go back through your vineyard to gather the grapes that were missed or to pick up the grapes that have fallen; leave them for poor people and foreigners. I am the Lord your God.

Leviticus 19:9–10 (GNB)

Notice how creation, community relationships and relationship with God are all interconnected.

The Old Testament Prophets draw out the link between Israel's treatment of those 'at risk' in her community and her relationship with God. When 'community care' is being neglected that is a sure sign that Israel has turned away from God.

There are many examples. Here is one:

You have oppressed the poor and robbed them of their grain. And so you will not live in the fine stone houses you build or drink wine from the beautiful vineyards you plant. I know how terrible your sins are and how many crimes you have committed. You persecute good men, take bribes, and prevent the poor from getting justice in the courts... Hate what is evil, love what is right, and see that justice prevails in the courts. Perhaps the Lord will be merciful to the people of this nation who are still left alive.

Amos 5:11–12, 15 (GNB)

Notice the *specific examples* of social injustice and how Israel no longer remembers how completely dependent on God she was when she herself was 'poor' in Egypt. She 'oppresses the poor', treating them as less than human. But God's justice works to restore the balance. Jesus takes up these Old Testament themes and tells us that he fulfils them in his own person:

'The Spirit of the Lord is upon me, because he has chosen me to bring good news to the poor. He has sent me to proclaim liberty to the captives and recovery of sight to the blind; to set free the oppressed and announce that the time has come when the Lord will save his people... This passage of scripture has come true today, as you have heard it being read.'

Luke 4:18–19, 21 (GNB)

Who are the poor, the captives, the blind and the oppressed in your local community? Talk together, sharing your reflections. Look at the concerns on your earlier list and see whether there are any links between them and what you have just been discussing.

How is the work of Jesus continued today? Talk together about the ways in which the Church works as a change-agent in your local community.

Moving on from here   *10 minutes*

What one step could you yourself take to begin to work for change in each of the two areas of poor quality care in your local community which you earlier identified?

You may wish to:

▷ write a letter
▷ find out more

▷ commit some time to pray regularly about it
▷ join with others to work for specific change.

What other steps could you take? Share your conclusions with each other.

Closing prayers

Place a lighted candle in the centre of the map of the local community. Then say or sing together:

> When I needed a neighbour were you there, were you there?
> When I needed a neighbour were you there?
> And the creed and the colour and the name won't matter
> Were you there?

Sidney Carter

Use a moment of silence to bring before God your main concern of the evening.
End by saying the Lord's Prayer and the Grace together.

MEETING 4

Family matters

THE FAMILY

Before starting someone should read through the Bible passages in the third section and decide which two will be looked at by the group. Members of the group could look at the others at home later.

Starting where we are   *25 minutes*

Someone should read this out:

What is a family? Here is one description:
 'The family is a group of people who are joined to each other by ties of blood or shared parenting and centred around more or less permanent partnerships of two people.'
 But the 'family' can take many forms. For example, among the Trobriand Islanders each man works to provide food for his sister rather than his wife. Tribal societies see marriage as the diplomatic uniting of two groups, more than of two individuals. However, the way that a mother protects and cares for her children seems to be a common thread.

Here are two lists of good and bad features of family life. (They were drawn up by a group of sixteen-year-old girls in a comprehensive school.) Read them through alone, or two people could read them aloud.

The best things about families:
You can be yourself—no pretence
Security—support—sharing
Love

The worst things about families:
Domineering parents
Emotional blackmail
Being expected to conform to family ideas

Extended family—wide age-group
Sharing responsibilities
Help you to learn—in every way
Good in time of crisis
You know they care
Practical support for each other

Gives you confidence
Enjoyment—sharing social events
Outings

Familiarity breeds boredom
Comparisons being made
Restriction on freedom
Dominance of one member—parent or other
Favouritism—not all children treated equally
Over-protection means you can't be
independent
Parents expect too much—over-ambitious
Interference
Lack of privacy
Lack of space
Conflict of interests
Irritating habits
Petty arguments

Look at the list of 'best things' and consider together:

If you were drawing up a similar list from your own recent adult experience, how similar would it be? Would you want to add anything?

Decide together what you think are the three most important elements of good family life.

Looking at the wider situation   *15 minutes*

Here are some facts about society in Britain today. Read them out round the group.
▷ Since the beginning of the 1970s young people have been marrying at increasingly older ages.
▷ During the 1980s there was a noticeable growth in the proportion of single women in the population.
▷ Marriage rates began to fall in the early 1970s and continued to fall throughout the 1980s. These sharp falls have been accompanied by a rise in the proportion of young people in cohabiting unions.
▷ There has been increased separation of marriage and child-bearing: since the beginning of the 1980s the number of children born outside marriage has more than doubled (though the majority of children are still today born to women in their first marriage). Figures published by the Central Statistical Office in 1993 say that 30 per cent of live births in the UK occur outside marriage.
▷ The average age at which parents start their families has been rising.
▷ There has been a trend towards the two-child family.
▷ There has been increased separation of child-bearing from child-rearing, especially for fathers. If the divorce rates for the 1980s continue, then 37 per cent of marriages will end in divorce and one child in five will experience a parental divorce by the age of sixteen.
▷ There has been an increase in single-parent families: in 1987, of all families with dependent children, 14 per cent were single-parent families. Most children live in a family headed by a married couple. However, the percentage of all dependent children living in lone-parent families has more than doubled since 1972, to reach 18 per cent by 1991.
▷ A substantial proportion of divorced people eventually remarry. Therefore many more children are now living in 'reconstituted' families involving step-parents.
▷ The population is getting older and there are more very old people. More children today are growing up with several grandparents alive and even great-grandparents.
▷ There are signs that the birth-rate is falling, which may mean that we shall soon find it difficult to pay for and care for our very old people.

Talk together to identify which three of these trends are having the greatest impact on family life in your locality. You may wish to include other trends which do not appear on the list.

Reflecting with the Bible   *25 minutes*

Choose two of the Bible passages. Read aloud one Bible passage and then spend some time talking together about the questions that follow the passage before passing on to read the second one.

Every year the parents of Jesus went to Jerusalem for the Passover Festival. When Jesus was twelve years old, they went to the festival as usual. When the festival was over, they started back home, but the boy Jesus stayed in Jerusalem. His parents did not know this; they thought that he was with the group, so they travelled a whole day and then started looking for him among their relatives and friends. They did not find him, so they went back to Jerusalem looking for him. On the third day they found him in the Temple, sitting with the Jewish teachers, listening to them and asking questions. All who heard him were amazed at his intelligent answers. His parents were astonished when they saw him, and his mother said to him, 'My son, why have you done this to us? Your father and I have been terribly worried trying to find you.' He answered them, 'Why did you have to look for me? Didn't you know that I had to be in my Father's house?' But they did not understand his answer. So Jesus went back with them to Nazareth, where he was obedient to them. His mother treasured all these things in her heart. Jesus grew, both in body and in wisdom, gaining favour with God and men.

Luke 2:41–52 (GNB)

What impression does this story give you of Jesus' family life? What are the good features? Do they have anything in common with the three important elements of family life which you decided on earlier?

[Jesus said,] 'You know the commandments: "Do not murder, do not commit adultery, do not steal, do not give false testimony, do not defraud, honour your father and mother."'

Mark 10:19 (NIV)

Do *you* think that to honour your father and mother is an important rule for living today? What do you think it might involve in practice?

Once when large crowds of people were going along with Jesus, he turned and said to them, 'Whoever comes to me cannot be my disciple unless he loves me more than he loves his father and his mother, his wife and his children, his brothers and his sisters, and himself as well. Whoever does not carry his own cross and come after me cannot be my disciple.'

Luke 14:25–27 (GNB)

What do you think Jesus is saying here about family relationships?

Children, it is your Christian duty to obey your parents always, for that is what pleases God. Parents, do not irritate your children, or they will become discouraged.

Colossians 3:20–21 (GNB)

So Jesus called a child, made him stand in front of them, and said, 'I assure you that unless you change and become like children, you will never enter the Kingdom of heaven. The greatest in the Kingdom of heaven is the one who humbles himself and becomes like this child. And whoever welcomes in my name one such child as this, welcomes me. If anyone should cause one of these little ones to lose his faith in me, it would be better for that person to have a large millstone tied round his neck and be drowned in the deep sea.'

Matthew 18:2–6 (GNB)

What status do children have in a family? Should they just obey? What does it mean to respect them?

Standing close to Jesus' cross were his mother, his mother's sister, Mary the wife of Clopas, and Mary Magdalene. Jesus saw his mother and the disciple he loved standing there; so he said to his mother, 'He is your son.' Then he said to the disciple, 'She is your mother.' And from that time the disciple took her to live in his home.

John 19:25–27 (GNB)

It is thought that 'the disciple he loved' probably refers to John. What did Jesus want John to do? Why did he choose John? Why was it so important to Jesus to make this request in the midst of his suffering?

From this incident, what do you think Jesus would have thought important about the family?

Moving on from here   **10 minutes**

Discuss questions 1 and 2:

1 How can individual family members help to bring about good family life?
2 What would you ask your MP or local councillors to do to help build good family life?
3 How could your church do more to strengthen family life?
4 What will you do: in your own family circle/in your church/in any other way to help your own family/other families to follow the teaching and example of Jesus?

Closing prayers

Someone can read out:

> *God our Father, your Son Jesus Christ grew up at Nazareth as a member of a human family. We ask your blessing on all the homes and families we know, and especially our own. Help us to follow the example of Jesus, as he cared for his mother, by loving and supporting each other, confident that we are secure in your love. In the name of Jesus Christ our brother. Amen.*

End by joining hands in a circle and saying the Lord's Prayer together.

(Before the next meeting, members of the group could look at all the Bible passages suggested in the third section and think about the other questions in the fourth section.)

No place like home

HOUSING

Starting where we are
15 minutes

Briefly describe your home, saying what is good and what is bad about it. Then, working in twos, fill in the following checklist, basing your judgments on your own experience:

	ESSENTIAL	IMPORTANT	NOT IMPORTANT
a room of your own	☐	☐	☐
television	☐	☐	☐
telephone	☐	☐	☐
a warm dry home	☐	☐	☐
good plumbing and electricity	☐	☐	☐
home ownership	☐	☐	☐
rent/mortgage not a worry	☐	☐	☐
safe, welcoming locality	☐	☐	☐
good neighbours	☐	☐	☐
access to work, schools, shops	☐	☐	☐
close to relatives and friends	☐	☐	☐
decorations you have chosen	☐	☐	☐
pleasing design	☐	☐	☐
comfy chairs and beds	☐	☐	☐
safe garden for children to play	☐	☐	☐
a guest room	☐	☐	☐
frequent visitors	☐	☐	☐
other…	☐	☐	☐

Now share with all the group what you have marked.

Looking at the wider situation
15 minutes

Take it in turns to read the following paragraphs:

There are over 12 million refugees in the world today, as a result of war, community violence, government repression, eviction and natural disasters. The majority are women and children.

Giana, a woman from Mozambique, had to flee the family farm when anti-government rebels came to raid. She says, 'They came in with their guns drawn, took our land, our food and most of the men and boys, including my husband, my son and my brother-in-law.' For several months she lived on the run with her sister Maria who was pregnant, hiding in the forest and scavenging for food. They managed to reach a hospital, where Maria gave birth to a daughter, but died in childbirth. Now Giana is waiting at the hospital with her orphaned niece to be placed in a camp for displaced persons.

In 1990 there were 167,000 households in Britain accepted as homeless by local authorities. Three million people, about 6 per cent of the population, have had an experience of homelessness in the last ten years.

Often local authorities want to spend much more to meet their local housing needs than central government permits. Recently one local council's housing strategy required expenditure of £40 million, but they were not allowed to spend more than £3.5 million. It costs more to lodge people in bed and breakfast accommodation than to build a house to put them in, but local authorities are forced to use bed and breakfast provision because of government restrictions on their housing budgets.

A young man was causing trouble at a drop-in centre for the homeless—not for the first time. The organizer said to him, 'Why do you come here? You don't like the place do you?' She was dumbfounded when he answered, 'It's the only home I have.'

'For £65 a week in London you can get bed and breakfast in a vermin-infested warren of rooms condemned as unfit for human habitation. Located in a crumbling block called — Villas in Hackney, it comes with damp walls, broken windows and leaking toilets. You get nailed-up fire escapes, empty fire extinguishers—and arson attacks. As landlord, Mr X collects around £3,000 a week from the 44 rooms. It is paid by Hackney Council and sent direct to Mr X's golf club.' (*The Independent*, 24 June 1990: Mr X's name and the name of the Villas was included but are not included here.)

Do you find any of these items surprising or shocking? What do you feel about this whole situation?

Reflecting with the Bible   *15 minutes*

Take it in turns to read the following passages from Scripture. They come from different times and different contexts and have been chosen because they link with the theme of 'home':

The Lord God planted a garden in Eden, in the East, and there he put the man he had formed. He made all kinds of beautiful trees grow there and produce good fruit . . .

Genesis 2:8–9 (GNB)

The Lord said to Abram, 'Leave your native land, your relatives, and your father's home, and go to a country which I am going to show you.'

Genesis 12:1 (GNB)

Share your food with the hungry and open your homes to the homeless poor.

Isaiah 58:7 (GNB)

Everyone will live in peace among his own vineyards and fig trees, and no one will make him afraid.

Micah 4:4 (GNB)

She gave birth to her first son, wrapped him in strips of cloth and laid him in a manger—there was no room for them to stay in the inn.

Luke 2:7 (GNB)

An angel of the Lord appeared in a dream to Joseph and said, 'Herod will be looking for the child in order to kill him. So get up, take the child and his mother and escape to Egypt, and stay there until I tell you to leave.' Joseph got up, took the child and his mother, and left during the night for Egypt, where he stayed until Herod died.

Matthew 2:13–15 (GNB)

Foxes have holes, and birds have nests, but the Son of Man has nowhere to lie down and rest.

Matthew 8:20 (GNB)

As Jesus and his disciples went on their way, he came to a village where a woman named Martha welcomed him in her home.

Luke 10:38 (GNB)

There are many rooms in my Father's house, and I am going to prepare a place for you.
John 14:2 (GNB)

From Paul, a prisoner for the sake of Christ Jesus, and from our brother Timothy—To our friend and fellow-worker Philemon, and the church that meets in your house.

Philemon 1–2 (GNB)

I heard a loud voice speaking from the throne: 'Now God's home is with mankind! He will live with them, and they shall be his people.'

Revelation 21:3 (GNB)

Which verses say something about what a home should be like? Are there any similarities between these things and the points you made on your checklist?

Which verses challenge us? How do they challenge us?

Moving on from here   *15 minutes*

As we go away from here and back to our own homes, it is good to take away with us from this meeting something to remember from looking at the wider situation (write this in the house shape), and something to remember from reflecting with the Bible (write this in the book shape).

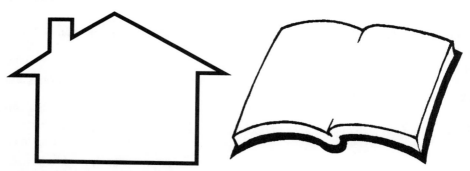

If you wish, and if there is time, you can share what you have written with your neighbour or with the whole group.

What organizations are there that work to house people? What sort of help do they need from us? Is there anything we should do as a group to help their work? (One local drop-in centre asks for gifts of tea-bags, sugar, biscuits or soup.) Here are some names and addresses, fill in the local group if you know one:

Shelter
88 Old Street
London
EC1V 9HU

Catholic Housing Aid Society
189A Old Brompton Road
London
SE1 7RT

Christian Aid
PO Box 100
London
SW5 0AR

local group

Closing prayers

10 minutes

Light a candle if you have one, then sing or say together:

He came from his blest throne,
Salvation to bestow;
But men made strange, and none
The longed-for Christ would know.
But 0, my Friend,
My Friend indeed,
Who at my need
His life did spend!

In life no house, no home
My Lord on earth might have;
In death, no friendly tomb
But what a stranger gave.
What may I say?
Heaven was his home;
But mine the tomb
Wherein he lay.

S. Crossman

Reader 1:   *Let us remember how Jesus set aside his home in heaven, made the world his home and shared in the world's homelessness;*

Reader 2:   *how he was born in a stable because there was no room in the inn;*

Reader 3:   *how he lived as a refugee in Egypt when he was a child;*

Reader 4:   *how he shared in the life of a home with his family in Nazareth until he was about thirty years of age;*

Reader 5:   *how he left that house to travel for his work, and so had nowhere of his own to lay his head;*

Reader 6:   *how he left this world to prepare a home for us in heaven.*

Reader 1:   *Let us give thanks for our own homes, and ask God's help to find the right ways of sharing our homes with others. (A few minutes silence.)*

All: *Our Father . . .*

Would you believe it?

THE MEDIA

You will need one copy of a recent newspaper for each person present (they can be different dates).

Starting where we are   25 minutes

Someone reads out the following:

> These days we are all bombarded with *information* of all kinds. Whenever we watch TV or read a newspaper or magazine we are confronted by events and 'stories' from all over the world; other people's opinions; other people's dreams, fantasies and visions; persuasive advertising. What can we believe? What must we take on trust? When should we ask questions?

Activity 1

Open a copy of a recent newspaper and glance through it. Choose one headline that strikes you. In turn, read out your headline, and everyone else gives a one-sentence 'knee-jerk' reaction to it (for example, 'How amazing', 'I don't believe that', 'How horrible', and so on).

Then briefly share your ideas together about the *purpose* of the writer in using each of those headlines.

Activity 2

Take a few minutes on your own looking at the following list and putting a number by each item, 0–5 to grade it in terms of its trustworthiness. 0 = not at all trustworthy, 5 = totally trustworthy.

.............a special TV broadcast by the Prime Minister

.............'Thought for the day' on Radio 4

.............a friend's account of a film s/he has seen

.............a live broadcast of a football match on TV

.............a report of a football match in a newspaper

.............a party political broadcast

.............an article in a woman's magazine on new developments in birth control

.............a radio play on the theme of abortion

.............a sermon in church explaining a passage from the Bible

.............a radio programme of poems written by a survivor from a major air-crash

.............a newspaper report stating that a particular item of food is now considered dangerous for pregnant women.

Talk together about what was difficult about doing the above exercise.

Looking at the wider situation

Take it in turns to read out the following statements:

Technological developments have greatly enlarged the scope, scale and character of the media.

World events are brought instantly into our homes.

The range of consumer choice—of newspapers, magazines and TV and radio channels—has been widened.

Commercial factors carry greater weight.

We are blessed with a free press; but freedom is often abused.

Greater speed of reporting may produce unbalanced and inaccurate 'stories'.

In a time of recession advertising revenue shrinks. Lower income from advertising may mean lower quality programmes. There may be a bias towards programmes which draw big audiences and against those that might be less popular.

The development of satellite TV is bringing even more advertisements into our homes, subjecting us to the persuasive powers and tactics of commercial advertisers.

Talk together about whether news is presented with truth and fairness when the selling power of news puts pressure on journalists to produce sensational or dramatic 'stories'.

Reflecting with the Bible

25 minutes

Someone reads the passage aloud or, alternatively, four people can share the passage by reading between them the parts of:

NARRATOR

THE ANGEL OF THE LORD/THE HOLY SPIRIT

PHILIP

THE ETHIOPIAN OFFICIAL.

An angel of the Lord said to Philip, 'Get ready and go south to the road that goes from Jerusalem to Gaza.' (This road is not used nowadays). So Philip got ready and went. Now an Ethiopian eunuch who was an important official in charge of the treasury of the queen of Ethiopia, was on his way home. He had been to Jerusalem to worship God and was going back home in his carriage. As he rode along, he was reading from the book of the prophet Isaiah. The Holy Spirit said to Philip, 'Go over to that carriage and stay close to it.' Philip ran over and heard him reading from the book of the prophet Isaiah. He asked him, 'Do you understand what you are reading?' The official replied, 'How can I understand unless someone explains it to me?' And he invited Philip to climb up and sit in the carriage with him. The passage of scripture which he was reading was this: 'Like a sheep that is taken to be slaughtered, like a lamb that makes no sound when its wool is cut off, he did not say a word. He was humiliated, and justice was denied him. No one will be able to tell about his descendants, because his life on earth has come to an end.'

The official said to Philip, 'Tell me, of whom is the prophet saying this? Of himself or of someone else?' Then Philip began to speak; starting from this passage of scripture, he told him the Good News about Jesus. As they travelled down the road, they came to a place where there was some water, and the official said, 'Here is some water. What is to keep me from being baptized?' Philip said to him, 'You may be baptized if you believe with all your heart.' 'I do,' he answered; 'I believe that Jesus Christ is the Son of God.' The official ordered the carriage to stop, and both Philip and the official went down into the water, and Philip baptized him. When they came up out of the water, the Spirit of the Lord took Philip away. The official did not see him again, but continued on his way, full of joy. Philip found himself in Azotus; he went on to Caesarea, and on the way he preached the Good News in every town.

Acts 8:26–40 (GNB)

Talk in twos or threes about the following questions:

Who did Philip trust? Why?

Who did the Ethiopian official trust? Why?

What difference did what he had heard make to his life?

Do you think the people of Caesarea believed the 'Good News' that Philip preached to them?

Then talk all together to agree three or four *guidelines* for judging the trustworthiness of the items listed under *Activity 2*.

Moving on from here   *10 minutes*

Resolve during the coming week to look out for:

▷ one example of something you hear or read that you feel very unsure about believing and think about why this should be so. (This might for instance be a news item or a slogan.)

▷ one example of something you can believe, and go on to think out whether I will allow it to make any difference to my life. (This might for instance be an article, an advertisement or a sermon.)

You could decide together to bring your examples and reflections to the next meeting and briefly share them.

Closing prayers

Put the newspapers you used at the beginning in a pile in the middle of the room. Spend a few moments quietly thinking about what you have discovered during this time together.

Then one or two people could read these prayers:

Loving God, you have entrusted to men and women great power for good or evil through television and the press. We pray for all who work in the media (include the names of anyone known . . .). We ask your blessing on all who have influence over others: that their skills and gifts may be devoted only to whatever is true and good. Amen.

Help us to be alert to distinguish what is true from what is false. Give us courage to follow the Way of Jesus Christ who is the Truth. We ask it in his name. Amen.

Almighty God, to whom all hearts are open, all desires known, and from whom no secrets are hidden: cleanse the thoughts of our hearts by the inspiration of your Holy Spirit, that we may perfectly love you, and worthily magnify your holy name, through Jesus Christ our Lord. Amen.

Spirituality and Christian Maturity

Growing and maturing in the Christian life
INTRODUCTION

Our heavenly Father wants us, who are his children, to grow up. The Bible makes it quite clear that Christians are supposed to grow up and mature in their faith, and we hope that these notes will be a help as we seek to do that. We are aware of a hunger in our church for the deeper things of God.

This material is not just for our heads. We shall get little benefit from it if we simply deal with it intellectually. We are to love God with all our heart and soul and strength as well as our mind, and the exercises in this course will affect the whole of us.

Here is an extract from Michael Green's foreword to John Wimber's *The Dynamics of Spiritual Growth*.

In the past two years [John Wimber] has surprised his enthusiastic supporters by taking conferences on leadership, prayer and holiness. And now he presents us with a book which reveals the roundedness and balance of the man. It is all about growth into spiritual maturity. It is positive and orthodox, generous and wide-ranging. He is disturbed at the enormous and accelerating erosion of Christianity in Western society in contrast to its remarkable growth in the Two Thirds World. He senses that hard times are coming, when external pressures upon the church will sweep aside a shallow Christianity. He sees around him in the church a sea of mindless enthusiasm on the one hand, and dead orthodoxy on the other: neither makes for a spiritual maturity which can withstand the negative tendencies of the end of the twentieth century, let alone evangelize effectively within it.

So he has written this book to help people grow from their current (fashionable) individualism and relativism into spiritual maturity. It is by far the most fundamental of his books: for it deals with the great core elements in the Christian faith—the nature of the God we worship, what he has done for mankind, the way of holiness in the modern world, self-sacrifice, servanthood and love.

A spiritual check-up

A quotation from Sister Margaret Magdalen:

> This [a spiritual check-up] may sound very introspective, but in fact it is just as healthy a practice as a physical check-up or the regular servicing of a car. The alternative is to live on the surface, drifting through life in a complacent unknowing. The human personality is a profound mystery and we can only know a very small part of the total truth about ourselves. In his merciful wisdom, God allows us only as much self-knowledge as we are able to bear at any given time, and even then he makes sure it is for our ultimate growth. This is actually the key word here—for any spiritual check-up has as its chief purpose, not a grovelling in sorrow (though sorrow may have a proper place in it all) but *growth*. Thomas Merton was fond of reminding his novices that sin at its nub is a refusal to grow. If we are to enjoy spiritual health, then we need to allow ourselves to be looked at by God. We may fear that divine scrutiny which pierces the very depths within us, but when we submit to it regularly, we come to realise more and more that, 'the love of God is broader than the measure of man's mind, and the heart of the Eternal is most wonderfully kind.'

The Apostle Paul is fairly sharp with Christians who have not matured in their faith. Read out 1 Corinthians chapters 2 and 3.

Discussion questions

▷ What is God's wisdom?
▷ What is an immature, unspiritual Christian like—and what is a mature, spiritual Christian like?

Exercise

(Note: each person should have a paper and pen.)

Read out Psalm 51:1–6. Then reflect in silence on the various aspects of your life and write briefly what comes to you.

▷ Think of your work: your relationships there, the quality of your work, and your commitment to it.
▷ Think about the Church, and your attitude to it and your feelings about it. Consider your relationships within it. What do you bring to the Sunday service? What don't you bring?
▷ Think about your relationships with your family—and with your friends.
▷ Think about your prayer life, and how much you praise God.
▷ Think about your Bible study and your knowledge of the Bible. Has it grown stale?

Then spend some time in silence, looking at what you have written, reflecting upon it, and continuing to pray that God, who desires truth in the inner parts, will teach you wisdom in the inmost place. As you do this, choose one area to start work in. Perhaps share this with the group. (You can take your thoughts home with you and continue praying about them.)

Finally, ask people to shut their eyes and listen as you read out Psalm 51:7–17.

SB

Keeping a spiritual journal

Keeping a spiritual journal can be a great help in our walk with God, and can assist our spiritual check-up.

What a spiritual journal is not:

▷ It is not a précis of the Bible passage for the day.

▷ It is not a lengthy, beautifully-written commentary in excellent English to be published in next week's *Church Times* or the *Church of England Newspaper*.

▷ It is not for public reading in any shape or form.

▷ It does not have to be written every single day.

So—what is a spiritual journal?

▷ It is private, personal and a pleasure to write (no one else sees it).

▷ Sometimes it is long, sometimes short.

▷ It gives expression to fresh images which emerge from deep inside a person as God's word is read, reflected on and prayed over.

▷ By writing things down, hidden, suppressed emotions such as anger, fear and resentment can come to the surface and so facilitate the healing process.

▷ It is a record of the Christian's walk with God, showing how God has led, blessed, corrected and loved.

Equipment needed: notebook or file. That's all.

Exercises

Read Malachi 3:16–17.

▷ 'Remembering' is recollecting and putting together 'different members' to make a whole. Get the group to *remember* what has happened to them in the past week/day/hour.

▷ Have some paper ready, and suggest each one writes a letter to God about some aspects of this, not giving a chronological account, but expressing the feelings experienced. Ask, 'What were you most aware of?'

▷ How was God present/absent in this? And what response did this produce?

▷ Members may then like to express audibly in the group, or in twos and threes, some of the things which have come to light.

Read Mark 5:1–20 (slowly).

▷ Write down any personal remembrances as you read this description.

▷ Then imagine yourself standing on the edge of the cliff with Jesus, and as the pigs rush into the lake hear him say, 'There goes your gloom, anger, bitterness, hate, and so on . . . and rejoice.'

Further exercises

Here are two further exercises which almost certainly will not fit into the home group time, but which could very usefully be done at home.

How would you like to be remembered?

▷ Write your own obituary notice. Write the kind of obituary which in your wildest dreams you would like to have.

▷ Allow your imagination to run free—it can be great fun, and can help you to get in touch with your spiritual life.

Write out your 'faith history':
▷ Jot down the salient points.
▷ Ask yourself—what has God meant in my life?
▷ Who have been the most important people for me?
▷ What have been the main events?
▷ Avoid self-judgment.
▷ Find God in your own 'history'. Be encouraged to go on trusting him.

JF

MEETING 3

Listening to God

We grow and mature in our Christian lives as we listen to the voice of God. But often when he speaks we don't hear. Read out Psalm 19. Discuss the two ways in which this Psalm says that the word of God is heard: namely through created things and through the written word. Ask two or three people to share how they have heard God's voice speak to them through the starry heavens or the earth and its creatures.

Exercise

Make sure everyone has paper and a pen. Lay out on a low table in the middle of the group the following objects:

a brown loaf (not a sliced one!)

a wine glass filled with red wine

a candle in a candlestick (light at the start of the exercise)

a small bowl of water

some fresh flowers in a small vase.

Ask each person to reflect on each thing and write down what it says to them. Then ask people to share with the group what they wrote.

Reflection

Read out Psalm 40:1–8. This is a messianic Psalm. Jesus always did the will of God because his ear was always open and attentive to listen to the voice of God.

Reflect on how Jesus used created things to point us to the creator. Read out Matthew 6:26–34. Discuss the reading.

Then read out Luke 15:3–7. What do these pictures tell us about God?

Read out Psalm 104:1–24 (very slowly) and ask people to be aware of their responses to the pictures which come into their minds. Afterwards, let everyone share their experiences with each other.

How could you improve your hearing, so that you let God's word enter into you and penetrate your being—and therefore change your life. Remember Thomas Merton in the first meeting: 'Sin at its nub is a refusal to grow.'

SB

A fresh look at Bible reading

A new, in-depth look at familiar passages will bring new riches to light. A fresh approach to the familiar can help when tackling the unfamiliar. So, here are some suggestions for the group, as well as for individuals on their own.

Entering into stories

▷ Spend a few moments settling down. Say a prayer such as Psalm 119:18, or the Collect for Bible Sunday (the first Sunday in Advent). Then ask God to touch you through the story, and give you the experience of the grace you need.

▷ As you will know the story well, let it speak to your heart rather than your head. Read it carefully several times, with lots of pauses, so that it can take hold of you.

▷ Put the Bible aside. Now sink into the scene: let it come to life with *you* as one of the characters. In your imagination take part in it. Notice the details, let yourself see, hear and smell the scene. Get caught up in the action.

▷ Let the drama slowly unfold. Let what happens happen. Don't control the story. Just allow yourself to be affected by it.

▷ Then, as your feelings are affected by the story, let yourself express these feelings to Christ. How does this touch your life? What do you feel moved to ask for, or to give thanks for?

The parable of the two sons (Luke 15:11–32)

The younger son (vv. 11–24)

Read the passage slowly (as outlined above). Suggest that each member imagines that they are the younger son. Then discuss together issues like these, and any others which emerge:

▷ I was longing to leave home—why?
▷ Why did my father give me all that money?
▷ I wonder how he felt when I cleared off?
▷ I had to hit rock bottom before I began to think (v. 17) and there was plenty of time to think . . . What did I become aware of?
▷ Whatever made me eat humble pie and go back home?
▷ Why was my father so pleased to see me?
▷ Why did he give me a party and all those presents?

This could be the spiritual journey of each person in the group, and members may like to share or pray about some of the issues which have come up, for example, what happened to me when I hit rock bottom?

The older son (vv. 25–32)

Again read the passage slowly and suggest that each member imagines that they are the older son, and discuss issues like these:

▷ Why was I so angry when my younger brother left home?
▷ Why was I so happy running the farm on my own?
▷ Why did I lose my temper when he came crawling back?
▷ Why was I so angry about all the celebrations?
▷ Do I still love my father?

The two sons

Now divide the group into two, some taking the part of the younger son, and some the older. See if the two groups can talk to each other, *recognizing* each other's good points (notice what they are), discussing their father, and seeing how they are going to live together in the future.

End the evening with a time of shared open or silent prayer as seems most appropriate.

JF

Praying without ceasing and the sacrament of the present moment

Read out 1 Thessalonians 5:16–24 and discuss.

What is prayer? Ask everyone to help to define it and write down their definitions. As well as our normal definitions, prayer is also the relationship itself between God and us. It is the open channel between God and us which is the listening ear (which hears the word of God and then does the will of God: Meeting 3).

How could we pray without ceasing? This is certainly not possible if our definition of prayer is simply asking. To praise and give thanks *in all circumstances* is a richer way to pray, and will deepen our prayer life. People testify that to praise God for everything transforms their life and their relationship with God. Perhaps some have read Merlin Carothers' book, *Prison to Praise*.

Consider this quotation from Frances Dominica, the Superior of the Helen House Hospice for children:

> I think that throughout life we yearn for something that we can't put into words. I see prayer as an ache: aching love, aching compassion, aching sorrow, aching joy, aching contrition—whatever it may be—a yearning and a reaching out. And I know that the yearning won't cease or be satisfied until we are one with God and face to face with him. I don't have a picture of what it's going to be like. I just know that there is a kind of drawing all the time, a drawing on, and that we will not find completion in this life. Tremendous blessings, yes, and tremendous happiness—so much to thank God for, and each moment to live wholeheartedly and generously and joyously. But nothing is ever quite complete. I see life after death as the completion of that for which we long. 'When I wake after thy likeness I shall be satisfied . . .'
>
> In *Drawing Near to the City: Christians speak about dying*, by Shelagh Brown

Read out Romans 8:18–27—and discuss along with Frances Dominca's definition of prayer.

Pierre de Caussade, who was spiritual director to a convent of nuns, wrote *An Abandonment to the Divine Providence* in the process of caring for them, and in it he spoke of 'the sacrament of the present moment'. A sacrament is an outward and visible sign of an inward, invisible grace, so de Caussade is simply (and profoundly) saying that we can encounter God in whatever is happening to us in each moment of each day—in the present moment—whether that moment brings sorrow or joy, beauty or ugliness.

Exercise

This is a hard exercise, and some people will dislike it. But it is easy to encounter God in something beautiful. Spiritual maturity is about meeting him in something distressing, and discovering that the unhappiness we are experiencing at a particular moment in time is a sacrament of the present moment, through which we engage more deeply with the living God.

Shut your eyes. Be still for a few moments. Then imagine seeing a dead cat which has been run over lying at the side of the road. (Stop to think...) How are you experiencing God in that? Think about God's gift of free choice—to drive too fast or to drive safely... Think about God's grief over our treatment of his creation. Now be aware in the present moment... Listen to all the sounds in the room... to the sounds outside... pay attention to one at a time. Open your eyes and be aware of what you can see. Focus on different things... different people... Be aware of what you can feel... the chair supporting you, the texture of your clothes. Be aware of anything you can smell... or taste...

Share how that was for you and finish with a time of open prayer.

SB

Listening and loving

This final study from Romans 12 is an attempt to enable us all to go from the secret of God's presence into the world of the 1990s—not leaving Jesus behind but being increasingly aware of the Spirit's activity in ourselves, and in the world around us. We are to be kingdom builders/makers/extenders, for we are following the King.

Listening to the instructions (Romans 12:1–8)

▷ What does it mean to offer myself as a 'living sacrifice' to God? In what way is this worship?

▷ I don't believe my mind can be transformed in a moment—so how do I set about it? How do I know when it is happening? Is it the task of a lifetime? Who can I ask to help me?

▷ What results should I expect to see as my mind is being transformed?

▷ Do I know what gifts I am to use in building/making/extending his kingdom?

Loving others (Romans 12:9–21)

So many points are covered in this section. Leaders may well wish to select the issues most relevant to their group. To discuss two is quite sufficient. Aim to be practical.

▷ How do we detect 'sham' love? How do we know when someone really cares?

▷ How are we to show our love to other people of all kinds, types and faiths?

▷ What is true humility (v. 10)? How can it be put into practice?

▷ Paul (vv. 10–13) selects many lovely qualities—which of them apply to me? (in all honesty and humility!) If I try to put these into practice am I in danger of becoming too extreme? So how do I work out a policy of moderation?

▷ How well do I cope with myself when faced with those who do not like me—and show it (v. 14)?

▷ The dictionary describes empathy as 'the process of entering into another's personality and imaginatively experiencing his experiences'. Is this (vv.15–16) what Paul means? How do I do it?

▷ Peace at any price (v. 18)? Is this the gospel message?

▷ Revenge (vv. 19–21). This is a strong emotion. How am I to cope with it? Do we need help sometimes? Can I trust God enough to leave it to him to sort the situation/person out, as well as me?

Prayer

So many issues have been raised that it would be good to leave plenty of time to pray, either in small groups, or as a whole.

Some groups may like a follow-up session on Romans 12, or on the course as a whole. To grow and mature in the Christian life is the task of a lifetime.

JF

Recommended books

Sister Margaret Magdalen, *A Spiritual Check-up*, Highland Books, 1990

John Wimber and Kevin Springer, *The Dynamics of Spiritual Growth*, Hodder and Stoughton, 1990

Faithful Stewards

CONTENTS

Why stewardship?

There is no entrance fee to the Christian community. You don't have to pay your way along the Christian road. For each Christian, his or her giving both of money and of direct action must arise not from external obligations, but from a personal relationship with God the Father through our Lord Jesus Christ. How much do you want to give?

During this first week, we shall be looking at this basic relationship, in order to discover what should motivate us when we come to decide what our level of giving should be. This is very basic, and some established Christians may feel that they have been here before. If so, fine. But you don't spend money on painting the window-frames if the whole building is subsiding because of inadequate foundations. Check the foundations first.

Monday Week 1

I believe in God the Father Almighty, Maker of heaven and earth.

Apostles' Creed

The creed summarizes our faith, and right at the beginning of the creed is the heart of the matter. God is the first principle, the cause, not only of human life but of our whole universe. This belief does not necessarily find itself in conflict with science. Scientists may tell us how they think that life began. They may suggest when and where. But the response of faith is to the question 'Why?' Why is there a universe?

Each week we join in the words of the creed and state our belief that God is the creator of everything, seen and unseen. It is an awesome thought. Mind-bending. Take time to think for yourself about the implications of that statement. Our concerns, heart-felt though they are, are for a tiny area of a planet which is by any standards a small part of the universe. Perhaps you have at some time had the use of a telescope to search the night sky. Each of us has on a clear night looked up into the sky and felt incredibly tiny. Yet that same God the creator is close beside you every step of the way, valuing you even in the unimaginable distances of space and time. To him, there will be no problem too great to deal with, no end to his patience and love. Gerard Manley Hopkins wrote:

> The world is charged with the grandeur of God.
> It will flame out like shining from shook foil

This perception of the greatness of God consoled Hopkins when he suffered depression. It can help to put our problems in perspective.

Prayer

We praise thee, O God. We acknowledge thee to be the Lord. All the earth doth worship thee, the Father everlasting. May we, too, join in the worship. Amen.

Further reading

Genesis 1

Tuesday Week 1

Have you not known? Have you not heard? Has it not been told you from the beginning? Have you not understood from the foundations of the earth? It is he who sits above the circle of the earth, and its inhabitants are like grasshoppers; who stretches out the heavens like a curtain, and spreads them like a tent to dwell in.

Isaiah 40:21–22 (RSV)

The poetry of the Old Testament has helped people to understand the incomprehensible for thousands of years, and among the very greatest of those writers is the poet who composed chapters 40–55 of the Book of Isaiah. He saw the implications for believers of their faith in God the creator. He lived at a time when the people of Israel were politically defeated and scattered away from their beloved country. Some had lost hope that God was powerful enough to be able to help them. They thought that God could not cope. The poet–prophet composed stirring pictures of God to rekindle their hope. God looked on the nations of the earth as 'a drop from the bucket'. He showed that for God nothing was impossible. He brought back hope to those who were in despair.

It is tempting to sit down and despair when we begin to think of the problems of poverty, pollution, political corruption, homelessness, breakdown of traditional family networks, drug abuse, cruelty, senseless destruction of the beauty of our environment—as those people did for whom these verses were originally written. Too many problems even for God to cope with. Perhaps he has tired of us. Perhaps he is overwhelmed.

The reason why God the creator comes at the beginning of our thoughts on stewardship is that we can remind ourselves of who is really in charge. We are not alone in our efforts to solve problems, whether local or national or global. We are on the same side as God, whose over-all power will be sufficient for every eventuality. As Isaiah puts it, 'Fear not, for I am with you, be not dismayed, for I am your God . . . For I, the Lord God, hold your right hand; it is I who say to you, "Fear not, I will help you" ' (Isaiah 41:10, 13).

Prayer

Lord, we give thanks for those in every generation who do not lose hope when confronted with trouble; but who retain and proclaim their faith in you to guide them and help them every step of the way. Amen.

Further reading

Isaiah 40–41

Wednesday Week 1

And God saw everything that he had made, and behold, it was very good.

Genesis 1:31 (RSV)

Sometimes Christians get the reputation of being a miserable bunch. They are seen as denying themselves pleasure and concentrating on the next world so much that they disapprove of this one. Yet our faith in God as creator should make us, of all people, the most eager to enjoy the beauty and goodness of this world of ours. Think of the most beautiful garden you have ever seen, or of your own garden (if you have one) on a day when it was looking at its best: the flowers so different and all so lovely; colour; scent; birds and animals among the plants; people relaxing and enjoying the scene.

Think of the depths of a tropical rain forest which most of us have now seen thanks to the television: variety, abundance, so many species living in wild profusion, so that we can only marvel. Art, music, literature, the kindness of strangers: all can make us stand and say, 'Behold, it is very good.' This is not a world where our souls are trapped away from God. This is the earth that God has given us to enjoy, and for many it is a land flowing with milk and honey.

We cannot deny that there are problems. But the basic creation is bursting with abundant life, so that everyone should find enjoyment and stimulation and encouragement to worship the creator. We are not made for sadness, but to be happy and grateful for all the good things of life. 'Make thy chosen people joyful.' Grudging acknowledgement of God, niggardly response to the magnificent complexity of our environment would be a poor answer.

Prayer

Praise God in his holiness; praise him in the firmament of his power. Praise him in his noble acts; praise him in his excellent greatness. Praise him with the sound of the trumpet; praise him upon the lute and the harp. Let everything that has breath, praise the Lord. Amen.

Further reading

Psalm 104

Thursday Week 1

The Lord blessed [Isaac] and the man became rich; he prospered more and more until he became very wealthy.

Genesis 26:12–13 (NRSV)

From very early times, people believed that those who found favour with God would be rewarded in material terms. Abraham was wealthy in animals and possessions; Isaac grew rich as a farmer; Jacob stole the basis of his herds from his father-in-law Laban and kept an increasing number of camels, sheep and goats.

The kings of Israel, like their contemporaries throughout the Middle East, were judged partly by the magnificence of their courts and their household. The greatest of the kings, Solomon, impressed all with his affluence, and helped Israel to be powerful during his reign. The importance of wealth to political influence can be seen in the account of Solomon's meeting with the Queen of Sheba (2 Chronicles 9). At a time when each nation worshipped its own distinctive god, the relative importance of the god was judged by the riches of his worshippers.

The possession of wealth brought with it responsibilities towards the less well off in the community, and it was part of the rich man's life as a worshipper to give help to the poor and the sick. There has always been a part of the Jewish/Christian tradition that enshrines this belief that God blesses those whom he favours materially. We can see an extreme and perverse example of this in the appeals of US 'televangelists' which urge viewers to send in money so that they in turn will receive a 'dividend from the Lord' for their good actions.

Less controversially there are the examples of Christian businessmen who grow wealthy and then use some of their profits for the benefit of their employees (the Rowntree family in the nineteenth century built model homes for its workforce). Today many large corporations devote (significant word that 'devote') some of their resources to charitable giving. This demonstrates a long-lasting sense of responsibility to share the fruits of affluence. 'Everyone to whom is given, of him will much be expected' (Luke 12:48).

A blessing from God in the form of prosperity always brings with it the need to respond appropriately.

Prayer

Lord, you have entrusted to us our possessions and our resources. May we fulfil the responsibilities which you have also given to us, so that whatever prosperity we may have may be used not only for ourselves, but for the benefit of those less fortunate. To the glory of God the Father. Amen.

Further reading

Psalm 1:1–3

Friday Week 1

It is easier for a camel to go through the eye of a needle than for a rich man to enter the kingdom of God.

Matthew 19:24 (RSV)

From what we saw yesterday, Jesus' hearers would have been profoundly shocked when they heard him say this, as they tended to assume that riches (honestly acquired) indicated the favour of God. But Jesus was not the first to sound a note of caution. The prophets had warned that the material prosperity of the northern kingdom—after Israel split into two states—distracted the people from their proper concern with justice and with the whole-hearted worship of God.

The offence was not in being rich, but in using those riches to subvert due course of law. 'I know how many are your transgressions and how great are your sins—you who afflict the righteous, who take a bribe, who turn aside the needy at the gate' (Amos 5:12). Amos used language which even in translation is strong to the point of insult—the rich men's wives are referred to as cows, and pictured lying idly on beds of ivory, drinking wines from expensive bowls and anointing themselves with the finest oils and perfumes (Amos 4:1). They had entirely forgotten, or were entirely ignoring, God as the source of prosperity.

Taken as a whole, Jesus' teaching does not show a man who cut himself off from the good things of life. He enjoyed his food and wine, he dined with men of standing in the community, he was consulted by rich and poor alike. But he did warn that a man who was wealthy might be lulled into a sense of false security—might forget that the proper relationship with God was the most important thing in his life. Self-satisfaction prevents the believer from coming to God with humility and with regret for sins committed. From that point of view, the poor and the sick are closer to God because there is no disguise for utter dependence upon God. They know that they cannot look after themselves.

Thought for prayer

'Where your treasure is there will your heart be also.' Where is my treasure, and what is it? What do I think about rich people and about being rich?

Further reading

Luke 12:13–34

Saturday/Sunday Week 1

Ask and it will be given you; seek, and you will find.

Luke 11:9 (RSV)

Reading

Matthew 7:7–12

We have looked at God as creator and God as giver of wealth and prosperity. As we reach the end of this study of the foundations of stewardship, we need to root firmly in our minds the relevance to ourselves of what we have been thinking about. God created the world; God created humankind; God created us as individuals; God is the source of all that we have, whether we inherited it, or worked for it, or were given it. As we say in the Communion service:

41

For everything in heaven and on earth is yours;
All things come from you, and of your own do we give you.

It is a basic human response, when we have received happiness and love from another person, to bring them presents. When the love is mutual that is not a way of trying to buy future kindness. Nor does it intend to impose burdens of obligations on the recipient. It just celebrates at that moment the gratitude of the person giving, for what he has received. Perhaps you remember giving a home-made present to a small child and watching the delight in the child's face. Perhaps you remember as a child yourself being given some wonderful present and responding in happiness. This kind of love-present is worth much more than just its financial price—it is literally 'priceless' because it is not bought but given.

Our response to God the creator should at its highest be a love-present. The financial value is unimportant. We give the best we can. And we do not do so in the hope of some favour in the future or fear of punishment, but because we have been given so much that we need to express our gratitude by giving ourselves.

That is the starting point when we consider what our response should be in stewardship.

Prayer

Almighty God, in Christ you make all things new.
Transform the poverty of our nature by the riches of your grace,
and in the renewal of our lives make known your heavenly glory.
Through Jesus Christ our Lord. Amen.

Leaders' Notes Week 1

1 God the creator. If you can, avoid an argument about whether God created the world in seven days, and whether the Adam and Eve story is literally true. Genesis 1, the lesser-known of the two accounts of the creation at the beginning of the Bible, is a poem intended for use in worship, probably written quite late in the development of the Old Testament literature to honour God the creator.

2 Science and faith are seen too often as enemies, but they were not always, and they should not be. Much of the knowledge contributed by science has benefited mankind enormously—for example, the improvements in medical care. Where we fail is to ignore the ethical implications of discovery. Man or woman's brain, no less than man or woman, is the creation of God. Not to use it to the full would be as perverse as refusing to use our legs to walk.

3 God gave humankind 'dominion' over the earth. Consider how far that warrants our use of animals and the environment, and what our responsibilities in return should be.

4 The existence of evil in the world. If God created everything where did evil come from? What about earthquakes, volcanoes, flooding and other things that are known to insurance companies as acts of God? This is a very sensitive area, and one in which many people have found difficult challenges to their faith. Free will, the ability of individuals to choose between right and wrong, must take some of the blame, but we have to acknowledge that the existence of undeserved suffering in the world is as sure as that of beauty. A time of silent or meditative prayer may be one way to dedicate a discussion which seems to be bogged down.

5 Prosperity as blessing or danger: the Luke passage which is recommended as further reading is very familiar, but look at verses 29–31: seek his kingdom first and all these things shall be yours as well. It is a question of priorities.

The response of faith

Last week's readings and thoughts concentrated on God as the source of all our created world. We share this understanding of human life with the Jewish faith from which the Christian faith emerged.

But, of course, we as Christians have an additional reason to be grateful to God. Not only has he given us life and the means of living, not only do we know because of that we must value the created world, but also God sent his Son to live as a man amongst us. The earth does not just reflect the creative goodness of God: it has been the scene of God himself in the man Jesus, sharing our human experience. We have an example of how believers should live their lives in total harmony with God. We can see how Jesus lived as a proper steward of God's generosity to humankind.

Monday Week 2

We have not a high priest [Jesus] who is unable to sympathize with our weaknesses, but one who in every respect has been tempted as we are, yet without sin. Let us then with confidence draw near to the throne of grace, that we may receive mercy and find grace to help in time of need.

Hebrews 4:15–16 (RSV)

The conflict between our aspiration and our situation lies deep in the experience of everyone. We are confronted by the values of a success-oriented society (not excluding the Church) by which we are expected to live our lives: a man successful at his chosen career, listened to by colleagues who respect his skills, earning enough to support a loving wife and attractive children in an expensive home. Enough time to spend helping a charity of his choice, a low golf handicap, or an improved effortless backhand. This is the recipe for fulfilment offered us by the spirit of this world. But what hidden emptiness does it often mask?

Social pressures on a woman are, if possible, even more intense: the recipe for success is the route of promotion and success at work and also success as wife and mother taking on the pressure of being 'responsible' for presiding at the heart of a smiling, loving nuclear family, with social poise to host dinner parties in the evening. This, too, is social pressure to play a role rather than experience the freedom we were created to enjoy, and is too often embraced uncritically by the Church. The reality is often that she is merely existing from day to day, never catching up with the tasks from yesterday, grumpy, exhausted and feeling entirely unappreciated.

At every age the expectations put upon us will be different. Parents expect their children to do well at school. Older people expect younger people to welcome the offer of their experience, which would be so useful to them if only they weren't so blinded by their youth.

In fact, we all fall short of our own expectations, let alone those that would be laid upon us. In itself, this could just be a mild disappointment, but if it stops us from fulfilling our potential as accepted children of God, because of feelings of inadequacy or a fear of failure, it is a real danger to our development as Christians. Being a Christian is not about feeling guilty at our own shortcomings. Unless we can come to a realistic assessment of our qualities, we are not going to be able to use them most effectively. Jesus in the Gospels lived amongst people as they were. No one was on their best behaviour when he arrived. Yet it was people just as they were whom he chose for his friends and disciples. They stayed ordinary. They argued. They had days when they understood what he was teaching, and days when they utterly misunderstood. They let him down. But he loved them constantly. Accepting God's love gives us a value way beyond the expectations we put ourselves under, as a church and as individuals.

As we look at our own lives, to see what response we can make to God for all that he has done for us, we must come to terms with what we are: perhaps too busy and therefore always tired; perhaps not in very good health; perhaps carrying bitterness from past events in our lives; perhaps lazy. God doesn't ask us to be perfect, but he asks us to offer who we are to him, whatever our limitations. And as we offer the different parts of our lives to him, we will see them transformed by his presence!

Further reading
Luke 4:1–13

Prayer

Just as I am, thou wilt receive
Wilt welcome, pardon, cleanse, relieve
Because thy promise I believe
O Lamb of God, I come. Amen.

Tuesday Week 2

One of the scribes . . . asked him: 'Which commandment is the first of all?' Jesus answered, 'The first is, "Hear, O Israel: The Lord our God, the Lord is one; and you shall love the Lord your God with all your heart, and with all your soul, and with all your mind, and with all your strength."'

Mark 12:28–30 (RSV)

Worship is natural to human beings. At a time when church-going is very much in the minority in this country, this may seem unlikely, but at special times everyone has within themselves a need to worship, even if they would not express it in quite those words. Look at the response of Liverpool football fans to the disaster at Hillsborough when more than 100 people were killed. The cop end at Anfield became an altar with football scarves and flowers taking the place of offerings on the altar. Look at the young couple with their first baby, who turn instinctively to the Church for a baptism even though they themselves may not have had any links with the Church. It is not hypocrisy. It is the desire to respond to a wonderful new beginning by marking it in worship. It is a need to give thanks.

We have to build into our lives a regular commitment to worship in church if we are fully to meet our need. Not that this in itself guarantees fulfilment. If you bring with you a closed mind full of resentments and imagined grievances, and sit cocooned in your preoccupations through a service, you will not really have experienced worship. We need to come into the presence of God thinking of nothing but God himself—to be taken 'out of ourselves'. Whilst this involves our emotions, it is not a showy emotional buzz, but a putting into perspective of God and ourselves. We need to be able to listen to new insights into our faith, and to grow through them.

We need to come together with other Christians to celebrate together our faith in God. Christians find different things helpful. For some it is joining in the quiet solemnity of an early morning Communion service, or an evensong, and finding in the smaller group gathered there a more congenial atmosphere. For others it is informality, close contact and loud music. But we do need to come together. Worship is essentially a corporate activity. The life of prayer of the individual should be built on the regular attendance at Christian worship. Whether it is in the largest and most majestic cathedral, in a church, or even in a home, worship is vital to us.

Prayer

Almighty God, you have built your Church upon the foundation of the apostles and prophets with Jesus Christ himself as the chief cornerstone. So join us together in unity of spirit by their doctrine that we may be made a holy temple acceptable to you; through Jesus Christ our Lord. Amen.

Further reading

Acts 2:38–47

Wednesday Week 2

A new commandment I give to you, that you love one another; even as I have loved you, that you also love one another. By this all men will know that you are my disciples, if you have love for one another.

John 13:34–35 (RSV)

'See how these Christians love each other,' outsiders said about the first Christians. The early Church was characterized by the care that all church members took of each other, meeting both practical and spiritual needs. The obligation lies on us still, and we must confess at once that it is an area of Christian life in which we have all too often failed. Some people may think that worship, and the way Christians get on with one another, and tomorrow's theme of prayer, are not directly relevant to the consideration of Christian stewardship. But they are at the heart of the matter.

People who have no direct knowledge of the Church judge it by the people they know who go to church. It's as simple as that. If you have a neighbour who claims to be a Christian but who rarely if ever attends the church and when he or she does, comes back critical of the service and of the other members of the congregation, that person is not going to think very highly of the Christian faith. It is not a good advertisement for a community practising the love and care of God. No amount of time spent on church committees, no amount of money donated, can make up for poor witness when it comes to practising our faith.

On a more positive note, nothing is more effective in sharing our faith than to start off by looking after people in small ways according to their need—not as a 'ploy', but to fulfil the promise we make each week to serve Christ in one another. As we become involved in an attempt in the community to put into practice our Christian principles, we shall become aware of a paradox. It would be fooling ourselves to think that the Christian Church has a monopoly of care. Non-Christians do a tremendous amount of work to look after the less well-off in the community, work which Christians may feel should properly be 'theirs'. If we take the opportunity to work alongside those who do not profess faith in God, but who nevertheless are practising the teaching of Jesus to love their fellows, we have another insight into the way in which faith lies at the heart of human nature.

Jesus told the story of a man with two sons whom he told to go and work in the family's vineyard. The first son said that he would not go, but in the event he changed his mind and put in a full day's work. The other son said that he would go, but he did nothing. Which, said Jesus, did what his father wanted? God's work is not limited on earth to those who openly call themselves Christians; God is served in every place where people give generously of their time and abilities to help their neighbours. It is our privilege to be able to join in this work, not to monopolize it.

Prayer

Lord, here am I. Send me. Amen.

Further reading

Luke 6:27–36

Thursday Week 2

After he had dismissed the crowds, [Jesus] went up on the mountain by himself to pray.

Matthew 14:23 (RSV)

Throughout the story of Jesus' ministry which we have in the Gospels, there runs the thread of Jesus' own prayers. At the end of the day, or early in the morning before the arrival of the crowds who came to be healed, or to see what wonders he would do that day, Jesus spent time alone with God. This was not instead of attendance in the synagogue or the temple—it was as well as public worship. As each of us considers what his or her response to stewardship should be at this particular time, we must consider it in prayer.

Jesus' own disciples found it hard to pray and so do we. They wanted to know how they should go about it and so do we. Jesus told them how, and his advice holds good for us today. Keep it simple.

As long as the traditional form of the Lord's Prayer was the only one used in worship, that prayer was the one which could with confidence be used in a group containing both regular church-goers and occasional worshippers. We have confused the situation with the ASB versions of the prayer, but still if any group is called to pray the Lord's prayer and given no further guidance, they will instinctively begin: 'Our Father, who art in heaven . . .'. The familiarity of that prayer has a great feeling of peace for so many Christians; but there is always the danger that familiarity will breed, if not contempt, at least inattention.

It has been pointed out that at each stage in a Christian's life, a different phrase in the Lord's Prayer will strike a chord with him or her, as if it were brand new. It will certainly take us all our Christian lives to be able wholeheartedly to enter into those much-loved words as our own prayer. At a time when prayer seems difficult, come back to the simplicity of that basic and beloved prayer and to silence. For it is in the silence that should surround our prayer that we may begin to hear what it is that God is trying to tell us.

Prayer

Our Father, who art in heaven
Hallowed be thy name.
Thy kingdom come,
Thy will be done on earth as it is in heaven.
Give us this day our daily bread
And forgive us our trespasses,
as we forgive those that trespass against us.
And lead us not into temptation
but deliver us from evil.
For thine is the kingdom, the power and the glory
for ever and ever. Amen.

Further reading

Matthew 6:5–15

Friday Week 2

May the goodness of the Lord be upon us; may he prosper the work of our hands.

Psalm 90:17

Worship, mutual care and concern, prayer: all firmly 'religious' topics. But the essence of stewardship is not to be 'churchified', but to translate into practical terms the truths we begin to glimpse as we go on as Christians. What we do on Sunday is only the beginning. Whether we spend the week in paid employment, or in studying, or in unpaid work in our homes, or well-earned retirement, it is in our everyday lives that the fruits of our faith will be seen. Work is the common lot of humanity, but it will make different demands on each of us. For some, their profession is challenging and stimulating, offering its own reward. For others, routine or repetitive work, or a clash of personality at work, may mean that working hours hang heavy on our hands. Some cannot work even though they would like to. Prolonged ill-health when there is so much we long to get on with is a sore trial.

It is in everyday life that Christians exercise the significant part of their stewardship. Every day is a test of our priorities, and how we allocate our money. Every day will offer some opportunity to reach out a helping hand if we look for the chance to do so. Over and over again in the Gospels, Jesus tells us that it is by what we do that God assesses our faith, not just by what we say. Particularly when a person is the only Christian at work, colleagues will judge Christianity by how he or she acts: stewardship in practice. And the situation is the same in a family where only one member is a church-goer: the rest of the family will see Christian behaviour as what that one family member does.

Prayer

Almighty God,
You have provided the resources of the world
to maintain the life of your children,
And have so ordered our life
that we are dependent upon each other.
Bless all people in their daily work,
And as you have given us the knowledge to produce plenty,
So give us the will to bring it within the reach of all;
Through Jesus Christ our Lord. Amen.

Further food for thought

Think how you deal with the problems you encounter in daily life. Do you feel helped by your faith in these difficulties?

Saturday/Sunday Week 2

If I have all faith, so as to remove mountains, but have not love, I am nothing. If I give away all I have, and if I deliver my body to be burned, but have not love, I gain nothing.

1 Corinthians 13:2–3 (RSV)

Stewardship is our love in action, in response to God's love in creating the world and in sending into the world for our benefit his Son Jesus Christ. There are no rules which we can apply to govern what our response must be; we must assess in worship, in prayer, and in the circumstances of our everyday lives what should be an appropriate response to God's love. This great chapter from Paul's first letter to the Christians at Corinth shows that motivation is the key, not a legalistic formula for giving.

God calls different people to different ministries within the Church. Some are called to be full-time workers within the structure of the Church, be it in the pastoral ministry, or youth work, or administration, or whatever. Others are called to work which seems to fit more easily with what we imagine is Christian—such as work with the ill and the homeless. Whatever situation we find ourselves in, we can give our lives in God's service. We as a church are called by God to enable the work of the gospel by supporting full-time Christian workers: indeed this should be a natural response for the Christian. God does not call us to give to 'the Church' whilst neglecting our human responsibilities—it is poor stewardship of time to spend so much of the week committed to church activities that there is no time to share the happenings of the week with one's family. God desires a balance of contributions, given out of love and building up faith.

Time, money, talents: the response of love.

Prayer

Love divine, all loves excelling
Joy of heaven, to earth come down.
Fix in us thy humble dwelling
All thy faithful mercies crown. Amen.

Reading

1 Corinthians 13

Leaders' Notes Week 2

1 'Being a Christian is not about feeling guilty at your own short-comings.' In any group there may be an individual who is entirely satisfied with their own performance, and with their faith. To that person, this may seem like an invitation to self-satisfaction. But it is almost certain that the majority in the group will have worries about their personal failures. Offerings born of guilt can never be good stewardship (nor will they be effective at 'buying off God's disapproval').

2 Worship: a discussion of how far our innate need to worship is met by the current services available in the church may be instructive all round. If agreement arises on a need which is not being met in your church, perhaps you could pass this on. But stress also that people can benefit by attending a service which may not seem very relevant to them. Ghetto worship is not what we are aiming at. The different services can help individuals at different times. Visiting an alternative service may be an enlightening process.

3 Getting on with other Christians: how easy do people find it? How can you respect other traditions when they sometimes do not respect our own traditions? 'I beseech you brother, in the mercy of Christ, consider it possible that you may be wrong' (Oliver Cromwell to a Christian opponent). Could we do anything to extend our accord with other Christians?

4 The group could work on intercessory prayers that would be appropriate for stewardship renewal. This may be easier done in a group than as individuals.

5 Work as a suitable setting for stewardship—do people think that the idea of stewardship is really relevant to their problems at work? If it is possible to discuss a specific job with real problems, this could be helpful, unless the person whose job it is feels got at (for example, everyone thinks they know how a Christian teacher should behave, but it's not so easy confronted with thirty disaffected teenagers).

6 The next weeks' courses will go on to look at time, money and talents, but hopefully the foundation is now clear: love given in gratitude for all that has been given to us.

What shall we give? Time

Monday Week 3

Now after John was arrested, Jesus came into Galilee, preaching the gospel of God, and saying, 'The time is fulfilled, and the kingdom of God is at hand; repent, and believe in the gospel.'

Mark 1:14–15 (RSV)

'The time is fulfilled.' These are the first words of Jesus which we have recorded, and they don't at first glance make a lot of sense to us today. So we tend to jump on to 'the kingdom of God is at hand'. But to the Jews who heard Jesus' words, they made a lot of sense—although they were startling. For centuries the Jews had looked forward to the time when God would fulfil his promises and come to the help of those who worshipped him. Too often we ignore the fact that Christianity is a historical religion, a faith rooted in time. At a certain time, God brought a group of slaves out of Egypt into the country now called Israel. At a certain time David and his son Solomon were kings of that tiny country at the peak of its political power. At a certain time, Jesus of Nazareth was born a descendant of David to claim that he in his ministry fulfilled all the promises made of a perfect successor to David. On a definite day, Jesus was put to death by the Roman governor. Three days later, Jesus' disciples saw him alive again and were galvanized into their work preaching the gospel of the risen Christ throughout the Roman Empire. These are not abstract principles; these events happened. We live in another time, but we are still within God's overall time-scale. Christian truth does not lie outside time (although we believe it will outlast time) but must be lived on a day-to-day basis by each Christian. How we spend our time will be an indicator of our faith in action. Particularly in our busy lives, the gift of time is one of the most precious we can present.

Reading

Ecclesiastes 3:1–15

Prayer

O God, teach us to view time in the light of eternity, and help us to remember that none of us knows how many or how few days may be left to us. So keep us faithful to our stewardship, that when our Lord comes, we may be found using our time wisely, and may merit his 'Well done'. For the honour of his name. Amen.

Tuesday Week 3

And [Jesus] came to Nazareth, where he had been brought up; and he went to the synagogue, as his custom was, on the sabbath day.

Luke 4:16 (RSV)

We have already observed that each Christian should worship regularly together with other Christians (Tuesday Week 2). This is not only to meet a basic need for corporate worship; it is also to show that we are publicly committed to the Christian Church, and it is to meet with other Christians. A church which is regularly seen to attract a large group of worshippers will command more respect in the neighbourhood than one which is almost deserted. It is easier for an outsider to come to a service if there are plenty of others coming through the door; and the more Christians who worship together, the more opportunities there will be for appropriate learning. Children are by no means the only ones who prefer to join a large friendly group rather than a half-empty quiet room where it seems as if all eyes are on the newcomer. This is not just a futile 'numbers game'. It is for mutual encouragement that all the Christians of a parish should gather regularly to worship God together.

Many people are very busy, spending large parts of the working week away from home and consequently valuing weekends as the only time they have with their family and friends. But even in the busiest weeks, it is part of the Christian commitment to devote time to coming to church. It is essential to weave into our lives that hour which demonstrates our belief in what we say: 'We are the body of Christ.' Not everyone can afford large gifts of money. Not everyone feels that they have talents to put at the disposal of the church community (although we shall look later at this). But everyone can come and join in a service of their choice. It is our duty and it should be our joy.

Reading

Ephesians 4:1–7, 11–16

Prayer

We give thanks, our Father, for the unity which is already ours as Christians. We thank you that there is one body and one Spirit, one hope which belongs to our calling, one Lord, one faith, one baptism, one God and Father of us all. And we resolve that by your grace we may retain the unity of the Spirit in the bond of peace. Through Jesus Christ our Lord. Amen.

Wednesday Week 3

And the Lord came ... calling ... 'Samuel! Samuel!' And Samuel said, 'Speak, for thy servant hears.'

1 Samuel 3:10 (RSV)

Communication should be so simple. One person speaks, and another hears and understands. Yet each one of us knows that it is not always so straightforward. The entire counselling industry has grown up through the inability of human beings to make themselves understood, particularly to their closest family. A parent tries desperately to get back in contact with a teenage child, but all too often past mistakes get in the way and there is no real conversation, but instead another argument. Husband and wife, locked into the routine of everyday life, can forget the joy in each other's presence which brought them together in the first place. And in the wall-to-wall noise of today's world— radio, television, cassettes, the telephone—we can too often forget to listen to God.

Consistent attendance at Christian worship can be the starting point for listening to God, but it is only the start. Just as space should (must!) be found in the day for talking to family and friends, so there should be some space available for quiet reflection. The renewed sense of calm which is there at the end of a successful holiday, when most of the frustrations of our lives have been left behind for a couple of weeks, shows that it is for our own benefit that we build in time to put life back into perspective. Although it used to be taught dogmatically that this breathing space or quiet time should be first thing in the morning, this will be best left to the individual to decide—it will certainly not be easy to learn to listen if you are about to miss the train or delay the school run.

Too many people now are afraid of silence; or if not afraid, at best uneasy. But silence can prove an invaluable benefit when we want to make the most of our time.

True communication is open-ended: by which I mean that you cannot guarantee what it is that you will hear. But if you listen, then what you hear will be for you alone. 'Speak, Lord, for thy servant hears.'

Reading
1 Samuel 3:1—4:1

Prayer
Father, as we turn aside from the busy world with its noise and distractions, quieten our hearts in your presence, that we may be still and know that you are God. Our God, now and forever. Through Jesus Christ our Lord. Amen.

Thursday Week 3
Not everyone who says to me, 'Lord, Lord,' shall enter the kingdom of heaven, but he who does the will of my Father who is in heaven.

Matthew 7:21 (RSV)

I remember going into a Christian bookshop several years ago, and asking the assistant for help in finding the book I wanted. She was one of the rudest women I have ever had the misfortune to come across. It is always irritating to receive poor service, but it seemed an additional insult that someone working in a Christian bookshop should be so unhelpful. It would be all too easy to collect similar examples of so-called unChristian Christians.

It would be easy but it would be dangerous. For Jesus is not inviting us to join in condemnation of those others who do not do what we want of them; rather, he is warning us that it is our own behaviour in off-duty moments, when we are not thinking specifically about Christian stewardship, that the reality of our belief is tested. When we have had a really bad day, when we are thinking about our own preoccupations, and someone approaches us for help, it is then that our quality is tested.

There is a record in the Gospels of the constant tension which built up between Jesus and the Pharisees, and we all too readily assume that they were hypocritical in their high religious standards. In reality, most were committed believers who put a great deal of time and energy into the observance of their faith; but their failure was to translate their love for God into a parallel love for their fellow human beings. Ultimately they rejected Jesus' teaching because he spent so much time amongst people they considered the failures of society that they thought he, too, was a sinner. They would have no association with non-believers, or with fellow Jews who did not come up to their standards, in case their purity was contaminated.

The original Ten Commandments began with the command to love God, and went on to command love for the neighbour. The first letter of John in the New Testament is quite specific on that point: 'If any one says "I love God," and hates his brother, he is a liar; for he who does not love his brother whom he has seen, cannot love God whom he has not seen' (1 John 4:20). For most of us, this is the most difficult challenge of all: to live all the time, all our lives, so that we are ready to take an opportunity of service if one presents itself.

Reading
Matthew 25:31–46

Prayer
Lord, help me to love people and not to condemn them. Amen.

Friday Week 3

Take heed, watch; for you do not know when the time will come.

Mark 13:33 (RSV)

The Gospels looked forward to the second coming of Jesus as an imminent possibility. Every day could be the last before Jesus came. We don't look forward with the same urgency as those early Christians to the second coming. The end will come. Either the end of the whole world, or the end of our own lives. If we could foresee what the future would bring, we would almost certainly order our lives very differently. A constantly recurring soap opera plot is that of a character who has contracted some unspecified disease and has only six months to live (these illnesses are mysteriously not painful or disfiguring, just fatal). That character will seek to strengthen his relationships with family and friends, to put his life in perspective.

There are stories in the Gospels which make very much the same point that if we knew when an important event would occur, we would not be caught unawares: the bridesmaids at the wedding who waited for the bridegroom's arrival, only half of them with enough oil in their lamps to light him to the bridal feast on his ceremonial arrival. The rich man who pulls down all his barns to expand, only to die in the night before he can begin rebuilding. The householder who was burgled, but who would of course have been on guard, if only he had known when the thieves were coming. 'If only' is a phrase which could be repeated in a thousand such disasters.

Jesus throughout his ministry warns us about 'if only'. The teaching is quite clear. We must be ready at any time to account for the state of our lives. No grievance must be allowed to fester, no forgiveness be left until it is too late.

Reading

Matthew 24:36—25:13

Prayer

Almighty Father, your Son our Lord Jesus Christ when he came amongst us brought pardon and peace; grant that when we shall see him face to face we may be ready to greet him, and enter into his joy. Through his own love. Amen.

Saturday/Sunday Week 3

Alice sighed wearily. 'I think you might do something better with the time than waste it.'

'If you knew Time as well as I do,' said the Hatter, 'you wouldn't talk about wasting it. It's him.'

'I don't know what you mean,' said Alice.

'Of course you don't,' said the Hatter, tossing his head contemptuously. 'I dare say you never even spoke to Time.'

'Perhaps not,' said Alice cautiously: 'but I know I have to beat time when I learn music.'

'That accounts for it,' said the Hatter. 'He won't stand beating. Now, if you only kept on good terms with him, he'd do almost anything you liked with the clock.'

Lewis Carroll, *Alice in Wonderland*

We all know how variable time can be: every moment spent waiting for a friend on a freezing street corner seems like twenty, while time spent on an absorbing hobby is over before you knew it had begun. In the context of stewardship, 'spending' is the correct way to think of how we use the time available to us; and just as in any other budget, at different stages of our lives, we have differing amounts of time available to spend.

A church congregation contains all ages, and people in all circumstances of life. There are those who have to snatch time from an impossibly busy schedule to fit their faith into their lives. It sometimes seems as if this is the only sort of Christian there is, but that is not so. Others have, perhaps, too much empty time on their hands with the passing of family responsibilities or employment. They can feel pushed aside when others talk of their myriad commitments. Yet the opportunity to review life in quiet and prayerful contemplation has traditionally been held to be a great Christian calling, and the perspective on life which comes towards the end of the Christian way is of value to the whole church.

God cannot be satisfied with our 'spare time'. Our commitment must be total. The time which we are able to spend each week actively helping the work of the church should be an iceberg: the visible tip of a much larger whole.

Prayer

This is the day that the Lord has made,
Let us rejoice and be glad in it.
O give thanks to the Lord for he is good,
For his steadfast love endures for ever.

Leaders' Notes Week 3

There used to be a very popular Victorian sampler design: 'Thou God seest me.' It can feel threatening to think that there is nowhere we can go that is out of sight of God. Do members of the group mind the idea of constant divine supervision?

1 The time is fulfilled: in most people's experience, there is a right time and a wrong time to make decisions. Should we bear in mind the right time when discussing our faith with others? Or should we take every opportunity to talk, even if we are not sure it is appropriate? How do we recognize when the time is ripe?

2 What do we as a church do about those who visit the church only at Christmas and Easter? This is a very touchy subject, as the last thing a discussion should do is to discourage the infrequent church attender from coming at all. What could we do to encourage more regular church-going?

3 Listening: the forgotten skill. Silence: the forgotten peace. Do people find silence threatening, and how willing are they to trust themselves to listen? What about those, especially the young, who delight in noise and activity? Is this good or bad? (Best tackled if you actually have young people there—it's too easy otherwise to talk about *them*.)

4 Designer labels are all the rage. 'Benetton' on T-shirts, store names on carrier bags, so that people are walking advertisements. Are we good walking advertisements for Christianity? Are we advertisements at all? What about those who put 'Jesus loves you' stickers in the back windows of their cars? Does this help anyone to accept the gospel?

5 Discuss with great care 'if only'. Most adults have some profound grief which they would have handled differently 'if only' they had another opportunity. What role does confession and absolution take in freeing us from past wrongs? Read Matthew 11:28–30. Are we really taking advantage of Jesus' invitation to cast all our burdens on him?

6 Too busy, or not busy enough—the problem of differing demands on our time. Respect those who may feel that they have too much time and too little they can do. It can sometimes feel that everyone has stimulating things to do and interesting people to meet except us.

What shall we give? Money

Monday Week 4

[Jacob said,] '... the Lord shall be my God ... and of all that thou givest me I will give the tenth to thee.'

Genesis 28:21–22 (RSV)

At the announcement of a stewardship renewal campaign, the automatic response is: the church is asking for money again. We don't actually have to form the conscious thought. It is there before we know it. If these Bible studies are of any use at all, they are to demonstrate that a financial contribution, no matter how generous, is not sufficient to discharge our obligation to the church. But, of course, money is a vital part of stewardship. The church does need money, and much more importantly for each individual, we do have to work out how to handle our money responsibly, how to meet our own needs, and how to contribute appropriately to our Christian community.

Those who say that money is not important have one thing in common: they have enough money to live as they choose. Everyone who has ever been hard up knows that trying to live on insufficient means is stressful, leads to family arguments, and generally does not bring out the best in us. Christian stewardship of money will not bring with it an obligation to give away more than we can afford. Yet it must demonstrate that Christian giving ranks high in our priorities. Odd small change thrust into a collection box is not a recognition of gratitude to God for all that we are entrusted with.

To look at a rigid formula is a recipe for division and heartache. The biblical standard is a tithe—a tenth—of all wealth given for the support of the priesthood. It is an ancient commitment, mentioned first by Abraham (Genesis 14:20) and then by Jacob after he had experienced the presence of God at Bethel (Genesis 28:10–22). The tithe supported in their turns the two great temples at Jerusalem with all their attendant priests and workers. It provided food for the very poor. It survived until medieval times in England, as a form of payment for church lands. Yet the tithe pre-dates the modern state. At the moment in the UK, we have state-provided health care, education, law, administration and all the infrastructure of daily life which we take for granted until it goes wrong. We cannot ignore taxation, nor the high cost of housing, transport and other necessities. In view of this, some churches now suggest a guideline of not a tithe, but a twentieth: one-twentieth of income devoted to Christian giving.

It has to be said immediately that even some very committed families will not achieve this target. Nor will all that giving be channelled necessarily through the church, since many members of the congregation retain strong links with charities they support directly. To be unable at the moment to achieve that level of giving is not necessarily failure to exercise good stewardship. But there is an obligation on us—all of us—to think how we spend our money: to look at the budget and establish not how much is left over for God, but how much should be set aside for God.

Prayer

Guard us, O Lord, from the wrong use of money; selfishness, carelessness or waste; and from that obsessive love of money which is a root of all evils. Enable us to be good stewards of what is entrusted to us, to give or spend or save according to your will; so that neither poverty nor wealth may hinder our discipleship, harm our neighbours, or destroy our life. Through Jesus Christ our Lord. Amen.

Tuesday Week 4

Those who desire to be rich fall into temptation, into a snare . . . For the love of money is the root of all evils; it is through this craving that some have wandered away from the faith and pierced their hearts with many pangs.

1 Timothy 6:9–10 (RSV)

Being rich, like being middle-aged, is largely a matter of where you are standing. I was browsing through the bookstall at the Oxshott Christmas Fair last year when my eye was caught by the cover of a paperback. 'Do you sincerely want to be rich?' it asked. At exactly the same moment, the man standing next to me must have seen the book as well. Neither of us picked up the book. He grinned at me. 'Obviously we don't want to be rich,' he said. Very few of us would admit to a real desire to be rich. But to be a bit better off . . .? That would be lovely.

You don't need to be in touch with the pavement dwellers in Calcutta, or the children who scrape a living off the rubbish dumps of a South American city to know that all of us here, whatever the size of our bank balances, are rich in comparison not only with most of the people in the world today, but in comparison with most of the people who have ever lived. We have access to a variety of foods, we can travel, we live in comfortable homes, we enjoy incomparably better health than our ancestors. Yet we do not feel rich because other people have more than we do. Our unwillingness to recognize our own wealth can be an insidious danger.

Yet it is not true that the Christian Church is against the comforts and good things in life. It is not. There is no obligation on all Christians to be poor. But over and over again we are warned in the Gospels against the temptations of thinking that the possession of money or property can protect us from the realities of life and death. 'Money can't buy me love' sang the Beatles. It can't buy life or health or security in any real terms either. The danger is that we shall rely on what we can provide for ourselves, instead of relying on God.

Reading

1 Timothy 6:6–10, 17–19

Prayer

Lord, when we stop to think about it we know that money can buy us none of the things in life which we really value: loving relationships, peace of mind and the sure knowledge that we are acceptable to you through your Son Jesus Christ. Remind us when we are caught up in the making and spending of money where our true priorities lie. Protect us from the danger of wanting always just the little bit more than we have. Forgive us for all the times we fail to trust your promises. For Jesus' sake. Amen.

Wednesday Week 4

Remembering the words of the Lord Jesus, how he said, 'It is more blessed to give than to receive.'

Acts 20:35 (RSV)

We have looked at the dangers of regarding money as a safeguard. But there is a very positive side to wealth: we can give money for the help of our church community, and for those in need. The offering which we are able to make will strengthen the church for the work it has to do, both in the parish and in the wider world. By adding our contribution to church finances, we are taking an active role in fulfilling Jesus' charge to his Church to go into all the world to preach the gospel.

First and foremost, right here in the parish, we want to ensure that we have the material resources to function as an active, teaching and caring church. The roof must not leak, the lighting must be kept in good repair, the church must be warm and welcoming. Basic, yes—but it all costs money. Then the ministry must be funded. The pay of all Church of England clergy is fixed centrally and administered centrally; but it is paid for by means of the diocesan quota which is assessed according to the church membership. Some churches contribute not only sufficient for their own clergy but also enough to go towards the salaries of clergy in parishes where the congregations cannot meet the whole cost.

Each stewardship campaign plans for the following four years. This is because the life of a covenant approved by the Inland Revenue is now four years. Each church should be able to present its accounts to show that it has been a good steward of the money entrusted to it.

Reading

2 Corinthians 8:1–15

Prayer

Lord, we thank you for the opportunity of helping your Church to carry out its task. We thank you for accepting what we can give, so that the work of the Church is our work. And we give thanks for all those Christians who administer the Church's money and possessions to enable it to fulfil its mission to preach the gospel.

Lord, in your mercy, hear our prayer. Amen.

Thursday Week 4

Each one must do as he has made up his mind, not reluctantly or under compulsion, for God loves a cheerful giver.

2 Corinthians 9:7 (RSV)

As well as providing for the upkeep and expansion of our own church buildings and ministry, we also have a responsibility to give to Christians and Christian charities who work throughout the world to preach the gospel. Money for mission is as old as the Church itself: our reading today from Paul's second letter to the church at Corinth shows that Christians have always given to help the expansion of the Church. We do well to build strong links with the projects and organizations we support, so that our commitment can be not only a financial one, but also one of spiritual support. From Calcutta to Natal, from inner-city deprivation to children abandoned on the street, our money goes where we cannot. It is our privilege to be able to contribute to the work.

It would be tempting to idealize this work of mission, but what we know of the lives of those whom we support should teach us to be more realistic. Mission is not, and never has been, a bed of roses. It is tough working in alien cultures, and with severely deprived people. Even for the most scrupulous charity, it is easy for a particular project to go wrong: for money to go astray, or for people to abuse their trust. When we read of food aid being sold on the black market, or of trusted Christians breaking down under the strain, we are heartbroken and feel betrayed. But it is not an excuse for abandoning our commitment to giving. We must be meticulously careful which intermediaries we use to transmit funds, but the fact that there is corruption alongside poverty should never be allowed to distort our commitment to go on sending what we can to wherever there is the greatest need.

'Put your money where your mouth is' is an old, if not an elegant, adage. If we are sincere in what we say about helping Christians in all parts of the world, if we want in our own country to foster the work of the Church, if we really mean what we say, then we must demonstrate it in hard cash.

Reading

2 Corinthians 9:1–15

Prayer

O God, we are sometimes frightened by our world, its cruelty and corruption, its greed and aggression, and we look for a quiet corner where we can live out our lives in peace. But we know in our hearts that this is cowardice. Jesus our King has overcome all the dark forces of evil. This sinful world is the world he has saved, and we are called to make his salvation real and to show it to our own generation. Strengthen us, Lord, for this task, with the help of the Spirit and build up your Church everywhere in faith and love, that the world may be released from its bondage and enjoy the perfect freedom of your kingdom; through Jesus Christ our Lord. Amen.

Friday Week 4

[Jesus] watched the multitude putting money into the treasury. Many rich people put in large sums. And a poor widow came, and put in two copper coins, which make a penny. And he called his disciples to him, and said to them, 'Truly, I say to you, this poor widow has put in more than all those who are contributing to the treasury. For they all contributed out of their abundance; but she out of her poverty has put in everything she had, her whole living.'

Mark 12:41–44 (RSV)

Under no circumstances should it ever become general knowledge how much is given to the church under the stewardship scheme. It is the practice in some secular fund-raising drives to mark particularly generous donations by a special roll of honour, or in some other way. That should not happen in the church. The treasurer will have detailed figures of covenants, but this information is strictly private. It is as a community, as a whole, that our efforts will see the light of day. All the contributions, both large and small, can be gathered together to be offered in a special service of dedication.

It is between God and each member of the congregation what the level of giving should be. God knows the commitments we each have. He knows the variety of circumstances which have brought us to our situation now. No pressure should be put on you from any member of the congregation to increase your giving. As you make up your mind how best to allocate your resources, take time to consider in prayer and silence how you should act. Then, when you have signed the cheque (or the banker's order, or the agreement to give weekly) it will be as much an act of worship as attendance at the Communion service.

Reading

James 2:1–8

Prayer

Lord, accept the money which I give as a response to your goodness. Let it be a sign between us that I recognize your generosity to me. Lord, I pray that this money may be used according to your plan; may our church play its particular role in the coming of the kingdom. We ask this for the sake of our Lord, Jesus Christ, who gave his life for us. Amen.

Saturday/Sunday Week 4

Render to Caesar the things that are Caesar's, and to God the things that are God's.

Mark 12:17 (RSV)

These words of Scripture are very frequently quoted, and almost none have led to such disagreement. Too often, it is assumed that Jesus was fixing an unbridgeable gap between 'religious' matters and 'ordinary life', so that the one was no concern of the other. In reality, Jesus was being asked awkward questions about paying unjust taxes to an alien dictator. The Jews had to pay dearly for their freedom to worship God according to their law; they had to pay in hard cash. Several leaders of would-be uprisings in the Roman Empire had encouraged the people not to pay their taxes, but to rise up and throw off Roman domination. Jesus, however, did not come to lead an armed revolt.

Paul followed Jesus in teaching that Christians should be law-abiding citizens. The early Church had enough problems confronting Jewish and pagan religious authorities without looking for trouble with the state as well. But it simply is not true that God does not care what we do with our money. The Gospels teach that in our dealings with money (as in our dealings with people) our real commitment to the gospel of love will be judged. Obsession with money drives out commitment to God. A true commitment to God will place all our financial dealings in their proper perspective. Paying taxes is a trivial necessity. Responding to God for his goodness is a full-time occupation.

Reading
Mark 12:13–17

Prayer
O God, whose Son Jesus Christ earned his bread at Nazareth by the work of his hands, and taught us that our possessions are a trust from you: help us to be faithful stewards of what you give; that in earning we may be just and honest, and in spending we may not seek our own good, but your glory and the good of others. Through Jesus Christ our Lord. Amen.

Leaders' Notes Week 4
It is very difficult to have a profitable discussion about money (what an apt turn of phrase!).

1 The members of the group are almost bound to be in very different circumstances, and opinions about the rights and wrongs of giving can look like criticism of a particular person, even when it is not meant as such. On the other hand, it is all to easy to be so abstract that the discussion loses all contact with reality.

2 The half-tithe (1/20th) mentioned in Monday's notes could seem threatening. I know that my own family will be unable to achieve this target until our student children have completed their studies; but it is at least an initial figure to debate.

3 Make sure that the very basic machinery of covenanting is understood: that the church can claim back income tax where a member of the congregation enters into a four-year commitment to giving and is a tax-payer. This means that the individual can give more than it actually costs him or her. It also gives the church a solid financial basis on which to plan.

4 The amount of money which we spend out of our income on particular items is one way of reflecting our priorities: we can't control the mortgage payment, but we can control, for example, the amount we spend on our leisure activities. It would be poor stewardship if our payment to the church ranked lower than our wine bill.

5 What do members of the group feel about 'Render to Caesar the things that are Caesar's, and to God the things that are God's'? Compare the message of the parable in Luke 16:1–13. There is no room for a double standard between things financial and the rest of life.

What shall we give? Talents

Monday Week 5

Lord all-knowing, you have found me; every secret thought and word, all my actions, all my longings you have seen and you have heard. Lord Almighty, you have made me, fashioned me to keep your laws: your design and your creation—every part of me is yours.

Based on Psalm 139

When it comes to the contribution we should each make to the life and ministry of the Church, we are full of plausible excuses. Someone else would do it better, I couldn't do it well enough, I'm really very busy, no, I'm not the right person. In this, we are reacting just as people always have when God asks them to do something for him. When Moses was challenged to lead the people of Israel out of slavery in Egypt, he was full of excuses: God said 'Now therefore go, and I will be with your mouth and teach you what you shall speak.' But Moses said: 'Oh, my Lord, send I pray some other person' (Exodus 4:12–13).

But we ignore one vital point. When we acknowledge God as creator, we declare our belief that we are created by God. Each of us is an individual whom God has made. Each of us has the abilities and characteristics which God knows and recognizes. For each of us, therefore, there is a job to do—which we can do—a job which can best be done only by us. It is part of the cultural background against which we have grown up that we too often under-estimate our abilities. We do not want it to be thought that we are self-satisfied. Even those who have demonstrated in their working lives gifts of organization, management and communication skills, hesitate to offer those same skills in the service of the Church. This mixture of real humility and laziness threatens the scope of what we can do as a church community.

Each church needs the help of all those who worship there to become the church that God intends it to be. Most of the jobs are not too demanding of time, and most do not require us to learn new skills. Spread throughout the congregation, the task becomes easier. And as everyone who has ever undertaken it will tell you: the more you contribute to the ministry of the church, the more you get out of it.

Reading

Psalm 138:1–8

Prayer

Lord, you have made me the person I am. Please show me what I can do to share in the ministry of your Church. Guide me, and help me to decide what you want me to do. I ask this through Jesus Christ. Amen.

Tuesday Week 5

Now when they saw the boldness of Peter and John, and perceived that they were uneducated, common men, they wondered; and they recognised that they had been with Jesus.

Acts 4:13 (RSV)

We are as God made us; but we can also grow as we take our part in the life of the church. Within a living church community, there is scope for people to change their role in the life of the church. As some grow older, they will play a less active part and contribute instead their prayers and experience. As others grow more mature as Christians, they may feel challenged to take on activities which they could never have dreamed of when they first came through the church door. There is no 'them' and 'us' in the church family. Parents who bring their children to junior church share with junior church leaders the responsibility of helping those children to grow up with a strong faith, and may later be able to use that experience by themselves taking part in the leadership of junior church. Those who join in intercessions share with the person leading those prayers the responsibility of offering them in worship and faith, and may in their turn feel able to lead the congregation.

We have a clear example in the Gospels of the ability of Jesus to bring about personal development that would seem impossible. Simon the fisherman was an impetuous follower of Jesus who learnt from his mistakes, and became the leader of the early Christian community in Jerusalem. Despite his faults, despite his denial of Jesus after Jesus had been arrested, Simon Peter grew into the rock on which the Church was built. As he lived closely with Jesus, he learned; and the limitations in his character were replaced by strength. If we spend time with Jesus, in worship and prayer, we shall be changed by his presence. Little by little, the work which we are able to do can help us to grow.

Our obligation at the time of each stewardship renewal, therefore, is to see what changes should be made, what growth we can look forward to, and what new tasks we can undertake.

Reading
Matthew 16:13–20

Prayer

Lead, kindly Light, amid the encircling gloom,
Lead thou me on;
The night is dark, and I am far from home;
Lead thou me on.
Keep thou my feet; I do not ask to see
The distant scene; one step enough for me. Amen.

Wednesday Week 5

So take the talent from him, and give it to the man who has the ten talents. For to every one who has will more be given, and he will have abundance; but from him who has not, even what he has will be taken away.

Matthew 25:29 (RSV)

There is no doubt that, strictly speaking, the parable of the talents should appear in Week 4's series of readings about money. A talent, as most people know, was a unit of money, so many modern versions of the Bible translate 'talent' as 'pound'. But it is rooted in our minds as the parable of the talents, and so merits its place here. Read the whole story. There can be little doubt that the master of the three servants did not act fairly. Presumably he knew the character of his three servants and gave out his money accordingly—but he was very harsh to the man who did nothing with the money but bury it in the earth. Are we supposed to reason that God, when we account to him for what we have been given, will be equally harsh?

Parables are not kindly fairy stories. They show humanity as it is, not as it should be. We recognize that there are people whom we meet who seem to have every quality we would love to have, and in addition are 'born lucky'. They have friends, and their friendliness attracts more friends. They enjoy their work, and because they are so enthusiastic, they are promoted to even more satisfying work. They are, in short, very like the servant with the talents who managed to acquire ten more. Equally, the person who is always complaining of boredom or isolation is not going to attract lively friends. It might not be fair, but that's the way it is.

We can only employ the talents we have; but we must employ them. Just as a healthy person who was suddenly confined to bed would lose the muscles he had built up and become gradually weaker and more frail, we, if we do not use the qualities we have, will gradually lose even what abilities we have. If, on the other hand, we concentrate on what is within our compass, we shall find that our horizons expand, and we are led on to what would have seemed impossible. In our own direct experience, we can demonstrate that 'to everyone who has will more be given, and he will have abundance'.

But is God really the stern master who will condemn us? Much of what Jesus taught is a warning of what will happen to people who choose to live their lives apart from God. He wanted to bring his listeners up short, he wanted them to be shocked into thinking. When we look at the use we have made of all that God has entrusted to us, we are forced to admit that we have made a mess of it. But the other side of Jesus' teaching was that when we admit that we need God, he is so merciful that he reaches out to forgive us all that we have done wrong. We deserve the punishment, but through the love of Jesus, we can receive the welcome.

Reading
Matthew 25:14–30

Prayer
Almighty God, by whose grace alone we are accepted and called to your service; strengthen us by your Holy Spirit and make us worthy of our calling; through Jesus Christ our Lord. Amen.

Thursday Week 5
The body is a unit, though it is made up of many parts; and though all its parts are many, they form one body. So it is with Christ . . . You are the body of Christ, and each one of you is a part of it.

1 Corinthians 12:12, 27 (NIV)

Like yesterday's reading, the parable of the talents, this passage from Paul's first letter to the Corinthians is very well known. Its influence is felt in the parish Communion each week: 'We are the body of Christ' and 'Though we are many, we are one body; because we all share in one bread.' Paul uses the picture of a human body to show that the Church needs all kinds of ministry if it is faithfully to perform its task.

So far, so good. We are familiar with the picture. But how far do we really believe it? How far are we prepared to accept that all ministries within the Church are of equal importance to God? Paul lists various jobs within the Church in 1 Corinthians 12:28–31. In the 1990s, we could add others: magazine deliverers, crèche supervisors, junior church helpers at all levels, coffee hostesses, typists, sidesmen, leaders of intercessions with the service, choir members, flower arrangers, people to look after the sound system in church, people to help with the confirmation classes, churchwardens, financial administrators. These are all 'ministers' and servants of the Church.

When we think of the list of indispensable helpers who join together to form the life and work of our church, is there not still a tendency to put too much emphasis on those visible

61

tasks which seem to take up a lot of time, and think that these 'important' jobs must be left to someone else? All jobs are important—the most routine alongside the most visible. Without the network on the ground which can pick up when a neighbour needs a visit, or can welcome with a smile a stranger who comes to church for the first time, the church just will not be doing its job properly. All parts of the body need to function smoothly if the person is to be called healthy, and it is up to each of us to make sure our church community is healthy.

A large number of people play some part in the life of the church. It should be everyone. By joining in, by playing a particular role, each Christian both contributes to and begins to benefit from being an active part of the body. As we have seen, it will not always be the same role which we play. Circumstances change, and what we do as a church changes too. There is training available for many skills, which can help to develop our latent talents. More than any other single step, the taking on of a duty within the church can change our attendance at church services from a routine into real worship; from being someone who comes to church, the Christian who contributes in some practical way becomes a member of the church.

Reading

1 Corinthians 12

Prayer

We are the body of Christ. In the one Spirit we were all baptized into one body. Let us then pursue all that makes for peace, and builds up our common life.
Lord in your mercy
Hear our prayer. Amen.

Friday Week 5

We are to grow up in every way into him who is the head [of the Church], into Christ.

Ephesians 4:15 (RSV)

A body which stays still, which never changes, and never develops, is—if not dead—at least very sick. The more we are prepared to shoulder our particular part of the burden of the work, the more the church can offer. More both to the congregation, and to the local community. Most of us, in our mobile lives, have seen or been part of different church congregations. Some are slowly weakening; each month, fewer people show up for the services. Some churches are vibrant. People bring friends and neighbours because they themselves enjoy worshipping there. A lively service does not necessarily mean loud electronic music and repeated choruses—although we should offer different styles of services for those who wish to worship in less traditional ways. A lively service is one where the worship offered is sincere, and the blessing received is recognizable, and it is available as much through a Prayer Book Evensong, as through an informal Family Service.

The aim for a stewardship renewal campaign is to grow in relevance to the residents of the particular parish. It is not about twisting people's arms to come into the church, nor bending their ears by doorstep salesmanship. Rather, we are trying to provide answers to the needs of our community. God knows the need. We can play our part in meeting it. Whatever other role we assume within the church, one role is the duty of each individual, adult or child. That is, to be prepared to say that we are members of the church, and that the church is valuable to us. Not in a loud or aggressive manner, but in such a way that our friends know that here is the way in, when they feel the need.

Reading

Ephesians 4:7, 11–16

Prayer

Almighty God, we give thanks for this our community. We pray for all who live here and are our neighbours; we pray for all who work here. May we never be ashamed of our church; let us live so that those who know us may recognize that we have been with Jesus. For his sake. Amen.

Saturday/Sunday Week 5

When I consider how my light is spent.
Ere half my days in this dark world and wide
And that one talent which is death to hide
Lodged with me useless, though my soul more bent
To serve there with my Maker and present
My true account, lest He returning chide;
'Doth God exact day-labour, light denied?'
I fondly ask; but Patience to prevent
That murmuring soon replies: 'God doth not need
Either man's work or his own gifts. Who best
Bear His mild yoke, they serve Him best, His state
Is kingly. Thousands at His bidding speed
And post o'er land and ocean without rest:
They also serve who only stand and wait.'

Milton, 'On his Blindness'

All stages in a Christian's life are equally valuable in God's sight. Who better than God to know exactly how we are feeling both physically and spiritually? Who more loving when a bitter experience has left us drained and unable to face the future?

There is a role for all Christians, even for those at a very low ebb in their Christian lives. Illness, stress, bereavement, loss, rejection can each in their own way strike a blow as deep as Milton's loss of sight. Membership of the Church does not provide a talisman against pain and loss in our own lives—why should it, when Jesus himself did not avoid in his life betrayal and ignominious death?

At those times when we have been badly hurt, it would be impractical to think of taking on new responsibilities. The duty then of a Christian is to keep on keeping on—to retain contact with the church, to keep up attendance at worship, so that wounds can begin to heal, and the lines to God are kept open. 'They also serve who only stand and wait.'

Reading

Matthew 11:28–30

Prayer

Almighty God, whose most dear Son went not up to joy but first he suffered pain, and entered not into glory before he was crucified: mercifully grant that we, walking in the way of the cross, may find it none other than the way of life and peace; through Jesus Christ our Lord. Amen.

The Collect for the Fourth Sunday before Easter (ASB)

Leaders' Notes Week 5

1 The primary aim of this week's readings is to encourage members of the group to take on whatever role in the community is best suited to them. Some people would not mind taking on a part in the service—reading the Bible or leading the prayers, whilst some others would find this intolerable, but would be quite happy to tidy the church mid-week, or make coffee after the service. We are not trying to encourage an unrealistic commitment—but we do want everyone to find a niche so that they feel a contributing part of the church.

2 Sometimes, it is easier to be asked than to volunteer. If you think that a member of your group is waiting to be asked, do please either ask them yourself, or pass a message to the minister.

3 When considering the image of the body with various parts, it might be helpful to remember that 'Christ has no hands but your hands, no feet but your feet.' This does not mean that each Christian cannot ask for help—it is possible to receive help, and still at the same time to contribute—he is the vine and we are the branches, needing to abide in him.

4 Do the group know all the different types of training which can be provided for junior church or Sunday School teachers, for pastoral assistants, Readers, or people who want to know more about their faith? Get the most our of your diocese and get in touch with it!

5 Saturday/Sunday's reading. Value the contribution of long-standing Christians grown older, who now make a largely silent offering. Their prayers are none the less valuable for that.

WEEK 6

Faithful stewards

Monday Week 6

Ask, and it will be given you; seek, and you shall find; knock, and it will be opened to you.

Matthew 7:7 (RSV)

As you have read the extracts from the Bible over the past weeks, and worked through the notes, I hope that you have felt again just how much we have to be thankful for. In all aspects of our life, there is so much to give thanks to God for; our response to him must reflect his own generosity.

It is a paradox that we seem to get more from the church as we give more to it in the sense of taking a more active role in it; and Christians who take on teaching, or helping with a church organization, will say that they do not regret it. To work as part of a team is a special privilege; friendship and fellowship grow alongside hard work and responsibility. Although we have looked at time, money and talents as different facets of Christian stewardship, the same principles are common to all. Because we acknowledge God in charge of our whole lives, we are encouraged to dedicate special time, money or skill for God. The offering which we set aside shows that the whole of our resources are entrusted to us by God.

That understanding, properly arrived at, needs to be brought to a service of dedication, and offered in worship at the beginning of this new period of stewardship. The chance to join in commitment and dedication gives us all new hope for the future.

Reading

Matthew 7:7–12

Prayer

Almighty God, Father of all mercies, we your unworthy servants give you most humble and hearty thanks for all your goodness and loving kindness to us and to all men. We bless you for our creation, preservation and all the blessings of this life; but above all for your immeasurable love in the redemption of the world by our Lord Jesus Christ, for the means of grace, and for the hope of glory. And give us, we pray, such a sense of all your mercies that our hearts may be unfeignedly thankful, and that we show forth your praise, not only with our lips but in our lives, by giving up ourselves to your service, and by walking before you in holiness and righteousness all our days; through Jesus Christ our Lord, to whom, with you and the Holy Spirit, be all honour and glory, for ever and ever. Amen.

A General Thanksgiving (ASB)

Tuesday Week 6

The Lord said to Moses, 'Speak to the people of Israel, that they take for me an offering; from every man whose heart makes him willing you shall receive the offering for me.'

Exodus 25:1–2 (RSV)

The decision which you make about what you will be able to make available—time, skills and money—is for you to make, and no one else. That it is a significant decision, again, is for you to ensure. All too often we allow our lives to be dictated by external events, rather than establishing what we actually want to do, until we are brought up short by a crisis and realize how much time we are wasting. The chance to stand back and assess priorities can put us back in charge of our time, in charge of how we live our lives.

The very wide range of readings which have made up the course over these six weeks may very well have opened up other ideas for further thought and reading. If this is so for you, there are a wealth of notes and guides available on various subjects, and you could explore further. Some areas for Christian concern may present themselves to you which you could touch on for their relevance to your whole Christian overview of life; an introduction to these areas is suggested over the next three days' readings.

But the main object of this course has been to bring together the threads which we can all weave into our Christian lives. The offering, blended from all of us, is to be given to God from our willing hearts. Not a tax, not an extortion, not a price to be paid—but a gift.

Reading

Romans 12

Prayer

Send us out in the power of your Spirit to live and work to your praise and glory. Amen.

Wednesday Week 6

Now the company of those who believed were of one heart and soul.

Acts 4:32 (RSV)

One of the greatest disappointments for the Christian is the division which exists within the Christian Church itself. This is not only a disappointment for Christians today—it has been a problem for Christians since the very earliest days of the Church, after that first wonderful burst of enthusiasm in Jerusalem, as we can tell from Paul's letters to the infant churches. We remember Jesus' great prayer for the Church, recorded in John's Gospel: 'I do not pray for these [disciples] only, but also for those who believe in me through their word, that they may all be one, even as thou, Father, art in me, and I in thee, that they also may be in us, so that the world may believe that thou hast sent me' (John 17:20–21).

It presents no faithful witness to the world to have Christians squabbling amongst themselves, when they affirm a gospel of love. The efforts of various traditions of Christians to reconcile their differences are recorded all through history. They founder always on the strength with which people hold their faith: if you believe something to be true, you cannot compromise on it. Now, in this decade, eminent church leaders from all churches are working together to resolve the profound truths into words acceptable to all. The ARCIC machinery has for ten years been bringing the Church of England to work more closely with the Roman Catholic Church. The new CTIE (Churches together in England) draws support from the Church of England, the Roman Catholic Church and nonconformists alike. All these initiatives are to be welcomed, and strengthened by action at parish level. In my own parish, we have happy memories over many years of shared worship in the Women's World Day of Prayer, as well as of other special occasions.

The theological causes of dispute are beyond most of us, and should in any case not be allowed to obscure our obligation: those who, like us, proclaim Jesus as Lord, as the only Son of God, are our Christian family, even though they worship in a manner which is not ours. When so many remain to be convinced of the truth of the gospel, it is madness, and a complete failure of stewardship, to spend energy arguing with fellow Christians. We have to learn to accept diversity while proclaiming unity—we have to learn to experience it in our own congregation, and we have to extend it into our dealings with other churches. Comprehensive Christianity—welcoming, and challenging, but always constructive.

People outside the Church are disgusted and bewildered by Christians attacking one another. They are quite right to be so. We have an obligation to do everything that we can, in prayer and in working with Christians of other traditions, to bring peace between Christians.

Reading

John 17:20–26

Prayer

O Lord Jesus Christ, who prayed for your disciples that they might be one, even as you are one with the Father: draw us to yourself, so that in common love and obedience to you, we may be united with one another, in the fellowship of the one Spirit. That the world may believe that you are Lord, to the glory of God the Father. Amen.

Thursday Week 6

And God blessed them, and God said to them, 'Be fruitful and multiply, and fill the earth and subdue it; and have dominion over the fish of the sea and over the birds of the air and over every living thing that moves upon the earth.' And God said, 'Behold, I have given you every plant yielding seed which is upon the face of all the earth, and every tree with seed in its fruit; you shall have them for food.'

Genesis 1:28–29 (RSV)

We began with creation, and in common with many other inhabitants of our world, we are increasingly preoccupied with creation. 'Green' issues—not the political party only, but the whole range of ecological concerns—are increasingly headline news. Should we be green Christians? The concept of stewardship here is crucial to the debate. God has given us the task of having dominion over the earth, which means being involved in the stewardship of all its resources. We ought to hand on the earth in good shape to our successors. Receive the estate, build it up where it is weak, protect its strengths, develop its resources, deliver it to the next steward or to the owner in as good or better condition than it was received—such is the job specification for a steward. Maximizing short-term profit at the expense of long-term prosperity is a recipe for failure.

The Church is an integral part of the human community. As such, it is influenced by 'fashions' in ethics and society. Yet the truths of the gospel are constant, and must be held secure and interpreted for contemporary audiences. This is the battle between tradition and relevance which ranges throughout Church history. Are we rediscovering the ancient truth of living in harmony with the earth, or are we distorting the gospel in an attempt to score cheap points in our secular society? We must always be wary of rushing in with the slick, disembodied biblical quote to jump on the bandwagon. There was a nineteenth-century clergyman who took the promise in Genesis quoted at the beginning of today's notes as a justification for his leisure activities. He shot animals, not for food, but because he enjoyed the sport. Those who now see the gospel only in terms of conservationist fervour stray to the other extreme of human perversity.

The interrelation between human patterns of life and the natural world is now backed up by scientific data beyond the dreams of those about whom we read in the Bible. But the truths revealed were not unknown to them. They habitually thought in a much longer time-frame than we do—they thought of their grandchildren and great-grandchildren. They valued the experience of their ancestors in farming and used that accumulated wisdom in their agricultural methods. They knew that it was worth leaving areas unharvested at the edge of fields, they knew it was better to plan a mixture of crops rather than rely on one alone, they knew that the land benefited from being left to lie fallow every few years. Many of the 'discoveries' which we are making—the dangers of over-fertilization, the importance of conserving water and keeping it uncontaminated—would have been self-evident to them. We can rightly point out in the contemporary conservation debate that there is a consistent biblical witness to sustainable use of the earth's resources. It's just a pity that we were not always vocal enough in proclaiming this truth!

We have to go on from here—it is pointless now to wrangle over the blame for pollution, and the devastating over-exploitation of land and sea. Each of us has a duty to inform ourselves of the problems, and to change our own lifestyle accordingly. It is not Christian behaviour to sip iced water whilst deploring the effect on the ozone layer of a million more Chinese acquiring refrigerators. 'Live simply that others may simply live' is an imperative for all of us.

Just as science has shown us that all life-systems connect, so all Christian truths interrelate. They are facets of the same gospel. Man was created by God, became polluted by sinfulness and lack of faith, yet has the potential to be redeemed through Jesus Christ. In a parallel way, the earth was created by God, mismanaged by generations of waste and destruction, but has the possibility of being restored by the creator. Paul, who of course knew nothing of our contemporary green concerns, had an insight into the completeness of creation: 'The created order waits with eager longing for the sons of God to be revealed ... in hope that creation itself will be liberated from its bondage to decay and brought into the glorious freedom of the children of God' (Romans 18:19–21). God the creator will ultimately be God the redeemer.

Reading
Romans 8:18–27

Prayer

'The earth is the Lord's and all that is in it' (Psalm 24:1). So we sing and so also we acknowledge. Yet we know, Lord, that while the earth is yours, you have appointed us stewards of your property. Keep us faithful to our trust; and make us mindful of our responsibility both to conserve the earth's resources, and to distribute its benefits justly and unselfishly, for the good of all people and for your great glory. Amen.

Friday Week 6

Man shall not live by bread alone, but by every word that proceeds from the mouth of God.

Matthew 4:4 (RSV)

Yesterday's introduction to the whole question of Christian stewardship for the state of the earth served mainly to show that this is an area for further study. If we are to be of any use at all in the debates, we must first know what we are talking about. Only then does the Church deserve to be heard. Within the Church are scientists, journalists, financiers, industrialists, doctors who deal with the illnesses arising from pollution and accident: the debate is not outside the Church. It is right inside our community. The special contribution of the Church, though, can be to lift the debate from a purely practical one to an ethical one. If we can inspire those working on the problem with a sense of mission, if we can encourage Christian young people to put their skills to the service of God's earth because it is God's earth, then we will be encouraging others to fulfil the particular role given to man and woman, that is one of exercising dominion over creation, because we are made in God's image.

This should be our aim: humankind fed not only equitably and with renewable resources, but humankind also recognizing its hunger for eternal truth. Jesus said: 'I am the bread of life; he who comes to me shall not hunger, and he who believes in me shall never thirst' (John 6:35). The perfect Christian steward asks for this bread of life, even whilst baking loaves in the oven!

Reading

John 6:1–14, 25–40

Prayer

We ask, Lord, your grace to help us live our lives every day in the strength which you supply, and in accordance with the principles we have been taught. And we ask, Lord, that we may never lose sight of your eternal kingdom, which in your goodness you have promised to us that we can share. May we work for the coming of that kingdom with the help of your Holy Spirit. Amen.

Saturday/Sunday Week 6

[Jesus] said to them, 'Come and see.'

John 1:39 (RSV)

St Andrew is particularly remembered in the Church for his role in bringing to Jesus his brother and his friend when he first met Jesus and realized his extraordinary power. Andrew did what is required of all of us: he shared his encounter with Jesus. Yet he played a relatively small part in the later accounts of Jesus' ministry, and was content for his brother to grow closer to Jesus.

In Andrew's ministry, we can celebrate the idea of Christian stewardship. He did what he could. He was not pushed beyond the role he felt called to. Not many of us are called to be leaders of the Church. But we are all called to our vital role in being there.

In 1991 the Church moved into the Decade of Evangelism. During this time there will be a concerted effort to re-open the lines of communication between those who are active church members, and the mass of the population whose religious experience is confined to baptisms, weddings and the occasional Christmas Communion. The gospel is not something to be kept safe within the Church: it is for everyone. As individuals, it is hard for us to see how we can be effective in bringing new people into the Church; but we are not to act as individuals. Our act of dedication at the end of this stewardship renewal campaign seals us as a Church community, and it is that community which can be effective in reaching out.

May we all be found faithful stewards of the gospel, which has been entrusted to us.

Reading

John 1:35–42

Prayer

Almighty God, who gave such grace to your apostle Saint Andrew that he readily obeyed the call of your Son and brought his brother with him: give us, who are called by your holy Word, grace to follow without delay and to tell the good news of your kingdom; through Jesus Christ our Lord. Amen.

Collect for Saint Andrew's Day (ASB)

Leaders' Notes Week 6

This week's readings serve both to tie up loose ends, and to point the way forward to possible new areas of exploration. You can, therefore, let the discussion take whatever path develops.

1 If there is any feedback about the course, or any disagreement with its general thesis, report back to whoever is organizing the stewardship campaign. Roughly speaking, it will have achieved its aims if members of the congregation feel able to put together for themselves a package of contributions—time, money and talents.

2 The area of what is a Christian lifestyle and what is not can be very differently interpreted by members of the same group. Housing and income have determining influences here. As in every other aspect of the course the preliminary thoughts on green Christianity are aimed at challenging people to think for themselves—not to launch into condemnation of other people's way of life. The applications of responsible stewardship of the environment are multifarious: picking up litter, being a careful dog owner, driving only when necessary, practical care for public open space and so on.

3 Conservation of the earth is important. It is vitally important. But it is not as important as confronting the challenge of the gospel. The bread of life is more important, because its truth is for all eternity—not just for today and tomorrow. We must not worship the creation instead of the creator.

4 Encourage attendance at a final service of celebration and dedication, because that will reinforce the message of Christianity expressed in commitment to worship and offering: a 'seamless' Christianity.

The Letter to the Philippians

CONTENTS

INTRODUCTION

The traditional view that Philippians was written from Rome in the early sixties, whilst not without its difficulties, is probably to be preferred to alternative suggestions that it was written somewhat earlier from Ephesus or from Caesarea. It is generally said that the chief theme of the letter is joy. This is because 'the word "joy" in its verbal and noun forms is found sixteen times in the four chapters' (R.P. Martin). But the reader quickly notices that the joy of which Paul writes is far from being a frothy, emotional matter; it is expressed in the midst of want, pain and uncertainty. It is perhaps better, therefore, to describe the chief theme not as joy but as peace—God's peace, established in Jesus and conveyed through his Spirit. It is this which makes possible the strange and improbable experience of joy through suffering.

Paul had five reasons for writing:

▷ to share news of his situation
▷ to thank the church at Philippi for their concern and help
▷ to combat false ideas that had troubled the Philippians
▷ to share with the Philippians his plans and hopes for the future
▷ to commune with his beloved converts in Philippi, who clearly occupied a very special place in Paul's affections.

The people of God— the nature of the Church

PHILIPPIANS 1:1–11

There is much questioning today about the nature of the Church. In what way is it special? In what ways (if any) is it different from any secular club or organization? In these verses, we discover something of Paul's understanding of the Church.

People and servants (v. 1)

The Church is the gathered 'people of God' because it is 'incorporate in Christ'. What exactly does this mean? Is 'incorporation' something we do? Or is it something that happens to us? Is everyone 'incorporate in Christ'?

Paul describes himself as a 'servant of Christ' yet he clearly served the Church. How is service of Christ related to service in and of the Church (or the world)? 'Bishops and deacons'—should there be any distinction between ordained and lay members of the Church? If so, what is this distinction and how should it be expressed?

Participation in grace (v. 2)

Characteristic of the Church is that it receives grace and peace from God. How do grace and peace manifest themselves in the Church's life?

Prayer to God (vv. 3–5)

Also characteristic of the Church is its life of prayer. Is the Church today a praying Church? Are we (as groups or as individuals) exploring new dimensions in prayer? Paul is speaking here not so much of intercessory prayer as of thanksgiving and rejoicing. How might we learn to emphasize these aspects?

Perfection in Christ (v. 6)

Christ is now at work in his Church and world; being the Church means having eyes to see this. Have we? Christ has further work to do; being the Church means having a vision for this. Have we such a vision? The perfection to which God will bring his creation (compare Ephesians 1:10) comes only at the 'End'; being the Church means not confusing Christian hope with a merely secular optimism. Do we confuse the two? With what consequences?

Partners in mission (vv. 7–8)

Since the Church is a community of love, there must be affection amongst its members. Paul even speaks of feelings of affection. Should there be emotion in our Christian relationships? Are there dangers in allowing some place for emotion? How does a congregation cultivate warm affection one for another? What does it mean, in practice, to share in someone's sufferings, particularly if all goes well with us?

Presented to God (vv. 9–11)

The Church has a destiny—to be presented to the Father as Christ's bride, the object of his high regard. Already this destiny should be creating within the Church genuine love and 'discrimination' (the capacity to make wise and balanced judgments). Are there signs of these qualities (growing) in your church? How can the Church work for the increase of these qualities without in the process becoming self-centred or introverted?

The proclamation of Christ—the nature of Christian witness

PHILIPPIANS 1:12–26

The Church's task is to proclaim Christ. The theme of witness is central to the biblical story, for God's work (however ambiguous) is never entirely hidden from men and women. God himself provides witnesses who can both understand his work and also declare it. In this study we see something of the character and content of this witness.

Christ's cause (vv. 12–13)

It was almost self-evident to the New Testament writers that the Church's witness would involve Christians in suffering. Why is this? Is there something essentially amiss with a Church which is not suffering? What forms might suffering take in our situation today? On what basis can we be confident that even affliction and persecution must contribute to the progress of Christ's cause?

Christ proclaimed—in sincerity (vv. 14, 16)

Two groups are mentioned: (a) those who being by nature timid have been encouraged by Paul's stand to grow bolder in their witness (v. 14). Are you encouraged by the brave witness of some individual? Can you yourself be an encouragement to someone less bold? (b) those who have appreciated the nature of Paul's case (that he was no criminal) and whose preaching therefore is based on understanding and is characterized by love. What does 'speaking the truth in love' mean in practice?

Christ proclaimed—insincerely (vv. 15, 17–18)

The situation was this: certain Christians were arguing that Paul's gospel was deficient, and so they preached partly in order to put him right. Are there comparable situations in Church life and witness today? Personal rivalry (v. 17) played its part; how can personality cults be avoided in the Church? Is Paul saying in these verses 'the end justifies the means'?

Christ shines forth (vv. 19–20)

Witness happens not only through words but also through lives. Do we concentrate on this aspect of witness sufficiently? For example does the Church fail in working-class areas basically because it witnesses with words whereas working-class culture is primarily not bookish? Notice that Christ 'shines' in response to prayer. Is prayer the most effective form of evangelism?

Christ alone matters (vv. 21–24)

Paul claims that for him 'life is Christ' (v. 21). This inevitably means:
▷ a subordinating of everything else (see further 3:7–11). What will such relativizing mean in practical terms?

73

▷ a certain 'world-weariness' (v. 23). Is witness our one reason for going on living? Should it be so? Is this an adequate appraisal of the world and of the purpose of living?

Christ is glorified (vv. 25–26)

How is Christ honoured in the faith of the Church and in its extension? 'To the glory of God' is written on static memorials; ought it to be the theme of all active witness? Can secular caring work also be described as 'to the glory of God'?

The pattern of Christ— the nature of the new life

PHILIPPIANS 1:27 — 2:11

In the course of an exhortation to unity Paul presents us with one of the most impressive theological statements of the entire New Testament (2:5–11; it may be that Paul is using an already extant 'hymn' to Christ, or he may himself have composed it). Here we find a wholly new pattern of living which calls into question the old 'way of the world'. It is the pattern of the survival of the weakest. It is the actualization of the policy stated in Mark 8:35—'whoever cares for his own safety is lost; but if a man will let himself be lost . . . that man is safe'.

The new life spells salvation (vv. 27–30)

To live according to the old nature leads to disintegration and death ('doom'), whereas to live the new life means 'salvation'. But what do these words 'doom' and 'salvation' mean in practice? Was Paul being unduly pessimistic about the 'old' order of things? Is there a clear-cut distinction always between those who 'contend for the gospel' and those who oppose it?

The new life involves unity (vv. 1–4)

Our new life is called our 'common life in Christ'. Do we agree that disunity is a scandal? Is there a 'common care for unity' (v. 2) in the churches today? How does this express itself? What does it mean, in practice, to 'look to each other's interests'? Is Paul asking the impossible?

The new life is in Christ (v. 5)

There is no new life independent of Christ. He alone explored the new way of living, following its pattern to its ultimate conclusion. We are called to acknowledge that he lived for us. But what does Paul mean by 'your life in Christ'? Does God see us as somehow in Jesus? If he does, then what is my 'actual self' about?

The new life means letting go (vv. 6–7)

Jesus' movement from on high to below is fundamental:
▷ for our understanding of God. Was the incarnation something alien to God's nature? Or does God's greatness consist precisely in his ability and willingness to condescend? What does it mean that Jesus 'made himself nothing' (literally 'emptied himself')?

74

▷ for our understanding of authentic life. Real life is not found through striving and acquiring and achieving, for despite these efforts we die. Why is it that we (and all creation) seem to have been made so self-assertive? What might it mean to 'make ourselves nothing'?

The new life accepts God's judgment (v. 8)

Christ died in obedience to the Father; even so, the Father seemed to abandon him. Why was Christ apparently God-forsaken (compare Mark 15:34)? If God seems to make decisions we cannot understand, do we react against them? Are we offended when he seems to answer prayer in ways we do not expect? If we we want God to be for us, must we somehow allow him first to seem to be against us?

The new life enjoys God's approval (vv. 9–11)

Christ's unique position of authority and power is bound up with his willingness not to assert himself, even in the face of what seemed like his Father's unfair disapproval. How should this pattern express itself in the Church's life (compare Romans 6:4–5)? Can we claim that Christ is Lord when there is so much sin and suffering in the world? Does belief in Christ's sovereignty affect our attitude to world events?

The purpose of discipleship— the nature of Christ's call

PHILIPPIANS 2:12–30

Paul's thought comes down to earth with a bump. What occasioned his moving theological exposition (2:5–11) was an exhortation to unity. What flows from it is a sober, practical reminder that Christ's new life must express itself in our ordinary, day-to-day living. There is no real theology which does not issue in ethical obedience and no really Christian ethic which is not founded on sound theological understanding.

The call to be active (v. 12)

'Justification by God' sounds good. But does it leave man in the position where it no longer matters what kind of behaviour he adopts (compare Romans 6:1–2)? Paul's answer is emphatic: we must earnestly strive as though our salvation depended on it! We must be active and deadly serious. Is there a special need in society today for the Church to emphasize and to exemplify obedience? Can we be active without becoming hectic activists? Can we be serious without becoming gloomy?

The call to be passive (v. 13)

Whilst striving as though his life depended on it, the Christian knows that it is all of God! So there is a need to 'be still and know that I am God' (Psalm 46:10). Is there a sufficient amount of this passive quality in Church life? How might it be fostered?

The call to uprightness (vv. 14–15)

▷ Christians are called to be uncomplaining. Are Christians noted for this uncomplaining quality? How can we encourage an accepting spirit in church life?

▷ Christians are called to be honest. Is this seen in the Church? Is it practical to try to be honest in a world in which dishonesty pays? What (for instance) would this mean for a Christian in business or for a Christian trade-unionist?

▷ Christians are called to be light. What light have we, as Christians, to bring to the world? Do we sometimes add to the confusion?

The call to sacrifice (vv. 16–18)

There will be pain and cost. What sacrifices, if any, are we called to make today in the interests of Church growth? Is the spread of the gospel making serious demands on us? Is the deepening of our own faith involving us in any cost?

The call to service (vv. 19–24)

Paul speaks now of his two colleagues. Of Timothy he says that he is (a) devoted to Christ, (b) faithful to Paul and (c) deeply concerned about the Philippians. How will the Church find, equip and sustain such men and women to serve Christ and his Church?

The call to acceptance (vv. 25–30)

Epaphroditus had been ill and had to be sent home. Would his home church reproach him with failure? The Church is called to be a supporting and accepting fellowship: is it? How can it be a gentle 'home for sinners' at the same time as being a rigorous 'school for saints'?

MEETING 5

The perfection of God's plans— the nature of Christian hope

PHILIPPIANS 3:1–21

In this third chapter of Paul's letter we find many of the themes of the 'hymn' to Christ (2:5–11) transposed into the experience of Paul and of the Church. The movement of Christ from on high to the lowly position of obedience and then back to the highest place, means that the Christian too must put aside his apparent 'wealth', his securities, counting them as nothing—in order to attain true glory.

Looking away from—false securities (vv. 1–7)

Paul knew that he had an impeccable pedigree and an impressive record, but he was willing to abandon it all. The gospel is for the poor (Luke 4:18); is there no good news for those who hold on to status, wealth and power? What does it mean to 'write off' all our assets (v. 7)? Does Paul mean that we must be ashamed of our heritage?

Looking to—true wealth (vv. 8–11)

Paul is clear that abandonment of 'wealth' leads not to poverty but to true gain. Are there signs of this true wealth in the Church's life? Does the Church dwell too much on the cost of discipleship and too little on the gain? What has the New Testament to teach about rewards?

Looking ahead—not back (vv. 12–14)

As though recalling Lot's wife, Paul refused to look back. The Christian is ever pressing on to new understanding and new witness. Is this restless pressing forward actually characteristic of Christians? If we have a tendency to be complacent, how shall we be stirred out of it? Is the sense of adventure in pressing forward part of the attraction in Christianity?

Looking for—growth in maturity (vv. 15–16)

What does it mean to become mature as a Christian? If there are different levels of maturity, how can an entire congregation be taught all together? Verse 15 speaks of God making things plain to us. How does he guide us into deeper understanding and fuller maturity? How can we be sure it is God guiding us and not someone or something else?

Looking at—an example (vv. 17–19)

Paul is not afraid to offer himself as an example to the Philippians. Are there any 'examples' (living or otherwise) to whom you look for encouragement and inspiration? Does this lead to the 'personality cult' we would wish to avoid? There are also examples to shun (vv. 18–19)! How can we describe someone as an example to be avoided and yet lovingly work for that person's forgiveness and renewal?

Looking upwards—for redemption (vv. 20–21)

Philippi was proud of its status as a free Roman colony. But Paul affirms that our true citizenship is in heaven. How is our loyalty to local society and to the nation affected by this higher loyalty? What is the relation of Christian discipleship to politics? Is there ever conflict between the claims of Caesar and the service of God?

Paul speaks of a transformation that awaits us at the End. How do we understand this? How important is Paul's emphasis (here and, for example, in 1 Corinthians 15) on the renewal of our body?

MEETING 6

The peace of Christ— the nature of God's gift

PHILIPPIANS 4:1–23

Jesus' farewell speech included the words, 'Peace is my parting gift to you, my own peace, such as the world cannot give' (John 14:27) and it is this peace (referred to in 4:7 as 'beyond our utmost understanding') that dominates Paul's thought throughout the several sections of this chapter.

Peace within the Church (vv. 1–3)

The case of a couple of women (it could as easily have been men!) at loggerheads calls for Paul's attention. Are we insufficiently troubled about petty squabbles that occur within a

Christian family or within a congregation? Why is it that paltry disagreements can sometimes wreak more damage than major rows? Are we able and willing to help in the work of reconciling (knowing that such folk often receive no thanks for their pains)?

Peace through prayer (vv. 4–7)

The reference in verse 5 is probably to Psalm 145:18; in prayer we are not crying into the empty spaces of a Godless universe, but are communing with the God who is always near to hear and to respond. What lessons about prayer and about a truly Christian stance in life do these verses teach us?

Peace through contemplation (vv. 8–9)

What are the things of worth upon which it is enriching to dwell? Can our list include all manner of aesthetic experiences (music, art and so on)? Can it include secular matters or must they be somehow religious? How, if at all, might we influence our society so that people might more readily see and hear things of worth?

Peace in our varying circumstances (vv. 10–14)

Paul believed that God is not only the Lord and giver of what we like, but Lord and giver also of what we would gladly avoid. But does contentment mean that we should never try to change society? Should we never try to improve things in the Church? What, if any, is the difference between contentment and passive resignation? What does it mean in ordinary living to 'have strength' even in (or especially in) weakness (v. 13)?

Peace and thankfulness (vv. 15–18)

Within his stance of calm content, Paul is certainly thankful to the Philippians for the help they had sent him. Why do we often find it hard to receive help and to be in someone's debt? Should gratitude be the dominant characteristic of all Christian living? How might gratitude be cultivated?

Peace be with you! (vv. 19–23)

Paul looks to God with expectancy (v. 19) and with praise (v. 20), and to his fellows with cordiality (vv. 21–22). How should the Church express its praise to God? Should worship become more 'hearty'? Or is praise primarily expressed in the kind of lives we live? How should affection within the congregation be expressed? Does the 'Peace' at Holy Communion help? Or, again, is it primarily in sober terms of practical care that love for one another is best expressed?

Walking in the Light

I like the confirmation responses. They are decisive: 'I renounce evil.' They are dynamic: 'I turn to Christ.' And they stress our relationship with God: 'I believe and trust in him.'

So when I was asked to produce a confirmation course for teenagers (at St George's Ovenden in Halifax, a fast-growing Anglican church in an urban priority area setting) I decided straight away to base it on those responses.

The resulting course is what lies before you now—'Walking in the Light'. Eight sessions: each one based around the responses your candidates will be asked to make; each one trying to make the link between liturgy and life—trying to narrow the gap between what we say on Sunday and what we are on Monday.

Each session has five elements.

You will find extracts from the confirmation service, to be read aloud. By doing so your group will familiarize themselves with what will happen at their confirmation.

You will find 'Keyword' exercises. These home in on one word from the confirmation service, and help the group to understand what it is exactly they are being called upon to say.

You will find 'Bedrock' exercises. These are all linked to passages from the Bible, and develop the link between the confirmation responses and themes in the good book.

You will find 'Lightbulb' exercises. The aim of these is to switch on a little light in the minds of the group—'so this is how this relates to me today'.

And you will find 'Connections'. These are to be done by the group members in their own time. They aim to encourage the candidates to develop their own private lives of prayer and Bible study.

As you use the course, please remember that these notes are only guidelines. The more that is personal, the more of 'you' that you can put into your leadership of this course, the better. Bring extracts from videos. Play latest chart hits that link in with the themes. Play album tracks that do the same. Do anything to bring this material alive in your own way.

And as you do, may God bless you and all the candidates you prepare for confirmation using this or other material.

By the way, when the notes say 'begin the session with' or 'end the session with', it goes without saying that you may top and tail the sessions with prayer and worship as is your custom.

Tim Mayfield

Keyword—'Turn'

1 Begin by reading out loud the section headed 'Renewal of baptismal vows'. You will see that for each week of the course, some of the wording of the service is printed. By reading each section out loud each time, you will familiarize your group with the words the bishop will say at their confirmation, and help them to have the experience without missing the meaning.

2 *Keyword.* Move next to the 'Keyword' section. Discuss each of the questions, perhaps under question 1 asking members of the group to share their story of a time when they got lost and needed to find the right way.

3 *Bedrock.* Now move to the 'Bedrock' section. Ask someone from the group whom you know to be a competent reader to read aloud the passage from Luke 19. The 'profile' section, question 1, entails each member of the group writing down four things about Zacchaeus (male, chief tax collector, wealthy, short, unpopular, able to climb trees, swindler, able to change, Jewish . . .). Once each member of the group has their four items, the group pools their ideas and builds up a profile of Zacchaeus.

   Tax collectors were hated because they collected taxes for 'the opposition', the Romans. They were seen as cooperating with an unwelcome foreign force, and into the bargain many suspected they were lining their own pockets.

4 *Lightbulb.* Using the key letter 'e' in every word, and using each of the other letters as many times as they like, group members try to find as many words as they can which describe things for a Christian to 'turn' away from: for example, lies, envy, hate, teasing, pride, theft, anger, greed, slander.

5 *Connections.* End the session by drawing the 'Connections' to the attention of group members. These are exercises to be worked through at home. For this first week, it might be as well to check that each member of the group is able to locate a Bible passage.

Keyword—'Repent'

1 Begin by reading once more through the section headed 'Renewal of baptismal vows'. You might like to invite the group to join in with their responses.

2 *Keyword.* Sin is 'walking away from God'. So 'repent' simply means 'turning round'. Illustrate this simply by using some object to stand for God. Then walk away from it—'sin', and then turn round—'repent'.

3 *Bedrock.* Ask a member of the group to read the passage as before. The 'profile' of the father is the same exercise as the profile of Zacchaeus. Each member of the group writes down four things about the father (two sons, kind, generous,

forgiving, compassionate, able to express emotion, loves parties...). Then pool each person's contribution and build up a profile of the father.

4 *Lightbulb.* On each of the scales, each group member places a cross to show where they are. Are they heading 'their way'—towards 'death'. Or are they 'with Jesus'? In terms of the story, are they still in the distant country feeding pigs? Or are they at home with the father? Or somewhere in between?

Once each person has completed the exercise, they could either explain their findings to their neighbour, or within the whole group, or both.

5 *Connections.* Finish by explaining the 'Connections' exercise, to be done at home in the group's own time.

Keyword—'Evil'

1 Begin by reading out loud the section headed 'Renewal of baptismal vows'. Explain that the three vows in this section form the first set of three responses the group will make at their confirmation.

2 *Keyword.* The four things the confirmed Christian is called to 'reject' are racism, violence, occult, and greed. It would be good to give an account of why they should be rejected, and of the effects of each. When I ran the course I interviewed onto tape a retired vicar who had experience of counselling a teenager frightened after 'successfully' using a Ouija board. I played the tape to the group, and we discussed it.

3 *Bedrock.* Once again, ask a member of the group, if they are willing, to read the passage from the Acts.

The 'profile' of Paul is the same as the exercises about Zacchaeus and the waiting father. Each member of the group writes down four things about Paul (Jew, strict Pharisee, opposed the name of Jesus...). Then pool your findings and build up a profile of Paul.

Although there is no documentary evidence to confirm it, my hunch is that Saul changed his name to Paul because he was unrecognizable as the same person after his conversion.

4 *Lightbulb.* If your group is large enough, break it into smaller groups and give each group one of the dilemmas for discussion. Then pool your findings. Develop the theme that sometimes it's quite hard to know exactly how to 'renounce evil' because difficult choices are entailed.

5 *Connections.* End by drawing the group's attention to the 'Connections' exercise to be done at home.

Keyword—'Father'

1 Point out that with the fourth meeting we begin to examine the next set of three confirmation responses. Read out loud the section headed 'Then the Bishop says...' and invite the group to practise their response.

2 *Keyword.* According to the confirmation response, God the Father made the world. Yet Jesus encourages us to call him 'Dad'. (Not 'Jacko', incidentally.) Under question 2 the group ticks the name Jesus invites us to call God.

3 *Bedrock.* Ask one or two readers (they could take a parable each) to read the two short parables from Mark 4.
  On the four lines the group jots down four things the two stories have in common: Jesus told them both, they're both about the kingdom of God, they're both about growth, they're both about seeds...

4 *Lightbulb.* Listed in the box are five arguments for the existence of God. Each group member scores each argument as to how persuasive it is. If they are really persuaded by an argument, they tick '9'. If they're not so sure, they tick '1'. When each person has finished, you could tot up your scores and see which idea is strongest for your group.

5 *Connections.* End by pointing out the 'Connections' exercise for the group to do in their own time. At about this point in the course you could be gently asking how people are getting on on their own, and finding out if habits of home Bible reading and prayer are beginning to take root.

Keyword—'Redeemed'

1 Begin the session by reading out loud the section headed 'Then the Bishop says...', asking the group to join in with their responses as before.

2 *Keyword.* The word 'Redeemed' is a tricky one. It's the most 'churchy' word in the six responses and needs to be understood. When we ran the course in Halifax, the group began to discover what the word meant by playing a game...
▷ Divide your group into two equal teams and put them at each end of the room.
▷ Each group nominates a 'victim', who is tied to a chair.
▷ Place a small ball in the centre of the room.
▷ Ask the first question from the quiz (see following questions).
▷ If a team member thinks they know the answer, they run and pick up the ball. Only accept an answer as correct if the ball is in the answerer's hands. (This is the fairest solution I know to the problem of 'I was first'.)
▷ If the answer is correct, give that person's team a coin. If it is incorrect, ask another question.

▷ When a team has five coins, they may use them to release their victim by 'buying him out of slavery'.

▷ The unfortunate victim of the losing team places their face in a bowl of chocolate Angel Delight. (Though careful with this one: when we played it, passions ran high and we ended up with chocolate Angel Delight all over the living room.)

When the game has ended, ask each member of the group to write in the blank 'Keyword' box what they think 'Redeemed' means. I wrote down 'being bought out of slavery'.

Quiz questions

1 Who invented the telephone?
Alexander Graham Bell

2 What is the first question a Bishop asks at a confirmation?
Do you turn to Christ?

3 What is five squared minus three?
Twenty-two

4 What is the name of the process whereby leaves grow by absorbing sunlight?
Photosynthesis

5 Jesus did not teach us to call God 'Denise'. What did he teach us to call him?
Father, or Abba, or Dad

6 Who commanded the British forces at the Battle of Waterloo?
The Duke of Wellington

7 Name the planet nearest the sun.
Mercury

8 Who wrote the play *Love's Labours Lost*?
William Shakespeare

9 What is the capital of Portugal?
Lisbon

10 Who was the first man on the moon?
Neil Armstrong

11 What 'm' comes before 'light', 'beam' and 'shadow'?
Moon

12 What is the third Gospel?
Luke

13 What is ten minus five plus ten plus three?
Eighteen

14 What is the third question a Bishop asks at a confirmation?
Do you renounce evil?

15 What are the Christian names, in order, of Laurel and Hardy?
Stan and Oliver

3 *Lightbulb*. The 'Lightbulb' exercise develops the idea of 'being bought out of slavery'. In the word square are ten theme words for the group to find. Read the passage below out loud, slowly, three times, emphasizing the words in bold. By the end of the third reading the group should have found all ten theme words . . . and have understood a little bit more about redemption.

Text for 'Lightbulb' word square:

In New Testament times **slavery** was very common indeed. Major towns would all have their slave **market** and rich people would go and buy someone to help with the household chores. If you were a slave, however, it was possible for someone to come and **redeem** you. A friend or relation would go to the slave **trader** and pay him a certain sum. You would then be redeemed: your redeemer would have bought you out of slavery into freedom.

    Paul uses the idea of the slave market as he tries to explain what he thinks the death of **Jesus** means. He says that we're all slaves to **sin**. We are bound in chains at the local slave market. Jesus comes, points to you and says to the slave trader, I'd like to redeem him/her. The trader replies, 'Certainly, sir, but the price for their freedom is your **death**. After quite a tussle in his mind, Jesus agrees, and pays the price on the **cross**. Because he did this, says Paul, I am no longer a slave to sin. I am free. I become instead God's **child**.

4 *Bedrock*. Draw out the contrast here. We have a choice: we can either be a slave to sin, or God's child.

    Question 3 is there to check that the group have got the basic drift of the session: that Jesus 'redeemed' us by dying on the cross, buying us out of slavery to sin.

5 *Connections*. End the session by drawing the group's attention to the 'Connections' exercise.

<hr>

MEETING 6
Keyword—'Life'

1 Begin the session by reading out loud the section headed 'Then the Bishop says . . .' Encourage the group to practise their responses, and point out that now we have the second set of three responses complete.

2 *Keyword*. The Holy Spirit is 'God' living inside a 'Christian', giving that person 'life'.

3 *Bedrock*. The 'Bedrock' exercise here is simple comprehension, so feel free to enlarge upon each of the questions to draw out the full meaning of the passage. If you have experience of the Holy Spirit working in your life, it would be good to prepare a simple testimony of exactly what happened to you, and what effect it had on you, to share with the group.

4 *Lightbulb*. As with 'renounce evil' I interviewed onto tape somebody talking about their experience of being 'baptized with the Spirit'. I find it helps concentration to use the different medium of the taped interview. After the tape, each member of the group placed a cross on the scale. This then led into discussion. You needn't have a tape, nor an interview, nor a testimony of course. The group could move straight on

to marking the scales.

5 *Connections.* End the session by drawing the group's attention to the 'Connections', and offer your time to anyone who wants to find out more about the Holy Spirit, or to ask any questions they might have.

Keyword—'Our'

1 Begin the session by reading out loud the section headed 'Then the Bishop says...' Point out that after the candidates have made their responses, the whole congregation joins in affirming their faith.

2 *Keyword.* Under question 1, draw out that a church is not a building. It's a family of people.

  Question 2: It doesn't say 'my' faith because the Church is more than a collection of individuals. It's a family, a team, an army.

  Question 3: The Church is more than just 'individuals'. This is something we do 'together'.

3 *Bedrock.* Under question 4, there is really no right or wrong answer. I put down that Paul's teaching on the body means that we're all 'different' and we're all 'important'. We all have a role to play in the local church, just like each organ has its function in the body.

4 *Lightbulb.* The 'Lightbulb' exercise helps the group to see ways in which they could contribute to their church. It goes without saying that you could tailor this to suit your own situation. Get each member of the group to tick at least one contribution. And if you're in a position to deploy this reservoir of talent... do so!

5 *Connections.* End the session by drawing the group's attention to the 'Connections' exercise.

Keyword—'Confirmed'

1 Begin the session by working through the whole extract from the confirmation service. If appropriate, take the group into church, show them where they'll stand, and do a dry run.

2 *Keyword.* The three situations point towards a definition of that word 'confirmed'. It means 'making definite something that was in doubt'. In this instance, it means that there was once some doubt about whether you would 'own' or uphold promises made on your behalf at baptism. Now you 'confirm' with your own mouth that you can indeed make these vows.

3 *Bedrock.* It would be good to have loads of visual aids to accompany this reading and attendant questions. Show the group the bread being broken. Show the group the wine being poured out. And so on. It would be good at this stage to take the group through the particular Communion service booklet that you use. Take nothing for granted and explain everything that goes on, giving the group a chance to come back to you with questions.

Again, if appropriate, it would be good to take the group to the altar rail, or wherever you receive Communion in your church, and actually show them clearly what happens.

4 *Connections.* The 'Connections' exercise is a 'Communion preparation kit'. Encourage the group to work through the preparation before their first Communion, and into the future, as a way of helping them to receive the most from this simple, deep and strange action.

Worksheets

1 The renewal of baptismal vows

The candidates stand before the Bishop; he says:
You have come here to be confirmed. You stand in the presence of God and his Church. With your own mouth and from your own heart you must declare your allegiance to Christ and your rejection of all that is evil. There I ask these questions: Do you turn to Christ?

Answer I turn to Christ.

Keyword: 'Turn'

1 If you realize you're going the wrong way, what's the most sensible thing to do?
2 What do you think it means to 'turn to Christ'?
3 Turning to Christ means turning away from something else. What is that 'something else'?

Bedrock

1 Profile: Zacchaeus _____
_____
_____
_____

2 Why were tax collectors hated so much?
3 What does Jesus 'say' to the crowd by going to Zacchaeus' house?
4 What does 'turning to Christ' mean for Zacchaeus?
5 What does Zacchaeus do that proves he's turned to Christ?

Jesus entered Jericho and was passing through. A man was there by the name of Zacchaeus; he was a chief tax collector and was wealthy. He wanted to see who Jesus was, but being a short man he could not, because of the crowd. So he ran ahead and climbed a sycamore-fig tree to see him, since Jesus was coming that way.

When Jesus reached the spot, he looked up and said to him, 'Zacchaeus, come down immediately. I must stay at your house today.' So he came down at once and welcomed him gladly.

All the people saw this and began to mutter, 'He has gone to be the guest of a "sinner".'

But Zacchaeus stood up and said to the Lord, 'Look, Lord! Here and now I give half of my possessions to the poor, and if I have cheated anybody out of anything I will pay back four times the amount.'

Jesus said to him, 'Today salvation has come to this house, because this man, too, is a son of Abraham. For the Son of Man came to seek and to save what was lost.'

Luke 19:1–10 (NIV)

Lightbulb

E	R	E	T	I
	A	N	Y	D
	L	G	S	P
	H	T	V	F

What should a Christian turn away from?

_____
_____
_____
_____
_____
_____

_____
_____
_____
_____

Connections

Read: Luke 17:11–19
Think: What might it mean for me to 'turn to Christ' today?
Pray: Lord Jesus, when I go my own way, I often end up feeling empty. Help me to turn round, and live my life for you. Amen.

2 The renewal of baptismal vows

The candidates stand before the Bishop; he says:

You have come here to be confirmed. You stand in the presence of God and his Church. With your own mouth and from your own heart you must declare your allegiance to Christ and your rejection of all that is evil. There I ask these questions:

Do you turn to Christ?

Answer   I turn to Christ.

Do you repent of your sins?

Answer   I repent of my sins.

Keyword: 'Repent'

1 What is 'sin'?
   LAWKING YAWA MORF DOG
2 What does 'repent' mean?
   RUNTING DROUN
3 'I repent of my sins' means that I turn to God, away from everything I know to be wrong.

Bedrock

1 Profile: The father
2 Who does Jesus think the father is like?
3 Do you believe God is like the father in this story?
4 What does the son do that shows he's 'repented'?
5 How does his father react when he gets home?

The parable of the lost son

Jesus continued: 'There was a man who had two sons. The younger one said to his father, "Father, give me my share of the estate." So he divided his property between them.

'Not long after that, the younger son got together all he had, set off for a distant country and there squandered his wealth in wild living. After he had spent everything, there was a severe famine in that whole country, and he began to be in need. So he went and hired himself out to a citizen of that country, who sent him to his fields to feed pigs. He longed to fill his stomach with the pods that the pigs were eating, but no-one gave him anything.

'When he came to his senses, he said, "How many of my father's hired men have food to spare, and here I am starving to death! I will set out and go back to my father and say to him: Father, I have sinned against heaven and against you. I am no longer worthy to be called your son: make me like one of your hired men." So he got up and went to his father.

'But while he was still a long way off, his father saw him and was filled with compassion for him; he ran to his son, threw his arms around him and kissed him.

'The son said to him, "Father, I have sinned against heaven and against you. I am no longer worthy to be called your son."

'But the father said to his servants, "Quick! Bring the best robe and put it on him. Put a ring on his finger and sandals on his feet. Bring the fattened calf and kill it. Let's have a feast and celebrate. For this son of mine was dead and is alive again; he was lost and is found." So they began to celebrate.'

Luke 15:11–24 (NIV)

Lightbulb

My way ←————————————→ With Jesus

DEATH   LIFE

Feeding pigs   At home with the father

Connections

Read: Mark 1:14–15

Think: In what ways have I 'sinned' today? How have I let God down, and hurt those around me?

Pray: Lord Jesus I have sinned against you today in many ways. I am very sorry. Please forgive me, and help me to begin again. Amen.

3 The renewal of baptismal vows

The candidates stand before the Bishop; he says:

You have come here to be confirmed. You stand in the presence of God and his Church. With your own mouth and from your own heart you must declare your allegiance to Christ and your rejection of all that is evil. There I ask these questions:
Do you turn to Christ?

Answer I turn to Christ.
Do you repent of your sins?

Answer I repent of my sins.
Do you renounce evil?
Answer
I renounce evil.

Keyword: 'Evil'

People who are confirmed declare their 'rejection of all that is evil'. Unscramble the letters to discover some things the confirmed Christian is called to 'reject' . . .

SMIARC
CLOIVEEN
LUCTOC
EGRED

Bedrock

1 In this passage, St Paul is on trial answering charges of being a 'trouble-maker'. In his defence, he tells his story . . .
2 Profile: Paul
3 What was Saul doing that was 'evil'?
4 What happened to him to lead him to 'renounce evil'?
5 What did he do that showed he had 'renounced evil'?
6 Why do you think Saul changed his name to 'Paul' in the light of his experience?

'The Jews all know the way I have lived ever since I was a child, from the beginning of my life in my own country, and also in Jerusalem. They have known me for a long time and can testify, if they are willing, that according to the strictest sect of our religion, I lived as a Pharisee. 'I too was convinced that I ought to do all that was possible to oppose the name of Jesus of Nazareth. And that is just what I did in Jerusalem. On the authority of the chief priests I put many of the saints in prison, and when they were put to death, I cast my vote against them, I even went to foreign cities to persecute them. 'On one of these journeys I was going to Damascus with the authority and commission of the chief priests. About noon, O King, as I was on the road, I saw a light from heaven, brighter than the sun, blazing around me and my companions. We all fell to the ground, and I heard a voice saying to me in Aramaic, "Saul, Saul, why do you persecute me? It is hard for you to kick against the goads."
'Then I asked, "Who are you, Lord?"
' "I am Jesus, whom you are persecuting," the Lord replied. "Now get up and stand on your feet. I have appeared to you to appoint you as a servant and as a witness of what you have seen of me and what I will show you. I will rescue you from your own people and from the Gentiles. I am sending you to open their eyes and turn them from darkness to light, and from the power of Satan to God."
'So then, King Agrippa, I was not disobedient to the vision from heaven. First to those in Damascus, then to those in Jerusalem and in all Judea, and to the Gentiles also, I preached that they should repent and turn to God and prove their repentance by their deeds.'

Acts 26:4–20 (NIV)

Lightbulb

In South Africa some groups of people imagine that other groups are inferior to them. Different groups have therefore had to live apart, use different facilities, and be educated separately. Black people are only now getting the vote. What will it mean for the South African government to 'renounce evil'?
You have a Saturday job at W.H. Smith. By an error on the computer you get paid twice one week. What does it mean for you to 'renounce evil'?
At the youth group at your local church, you discover that the coffee you drink is produced by very poorly paid peasants in Brazil. What does it mean for you to 'renounce evil'?
Wicksy is going out with Sharon. Cindy is married to Ian. No one knows, but Wicksy is the father of Cindy's baby. Wicksy knows, and still loves Cindy. What does it mean for Wicksy to 'renounce evil'?

Connections

Read: Luke 5:1–11
Think: Am I ready to 'turn to Christ'? To repent of my sins, like Peter did, and to 'renounce evil'? If so . . .
Pray: Yes, I am ready, Lord. Ready to follow you. Give me the strength to be a Christian, and to use me to change the world. Amen.

4 The renewal of baptismal vows

Then the Bishop says:
You must now declare before God and his Church that you accept the Christian faith into which you were baptized, and in which you will live and grow.
Do you believe and trust in God the **Father**, who made the world?

Answer   I believe and trust in him.

Keyword: 'Father'

1 According to the confirmation response, what did God the Father do?
2 What did Jesus teach us to call God?
   COLIN
   DENISE
   DAD
   JACKO
3 God not only made the world, but the entire universe. Yet the Bible encourages us to call him 'Father'.

The parable of the growing seed

He also said, 'This is what the kingdom of God is like. A man scatters seed on the ground. Night and day, whether he sleeps or gets up, the seed sprouts and grows, though he does not know how. All by itself the soil produces corn—first the stalk, then the ear, then the full kernel in the ear. As soon as the grain is ripe, he puts the sickle to it, because the harvest has come.'
The parable of the mustard seed
Again he said, 'What shall we say the kingdom of God is like, or what parable shall we use to describe it? It is like a mustard seed, which is the smallest seed you plant in the ground. Yet when planted, it grows and becomes the largest of all garden plants, with such big branches that the birds of the air can perch in its shade.'

Mark 4:26–32 (NIV)

Bedrock

_____

_____

_____

1 Why do you think Jesus says the kingdom of God is like a growing seed?

Lightbulb

	1	2	3	4	5	6	7	8	9
Things have a design, there must be a designer									
There must be more to life than what we can see									
Things growing from seeds can't be explained as an accident									
The world must have a beginning and an end									
Nature is too beautiful to be here by chance									

Connections

Read: Psalm 148
Think: In the Psalm, everything that God has made says 'thank you' to him. Watch out today for something in nature that makes you want to thank God.
Pray: Lord, there is so much to be thankful for. Help me to see your hand in all you have made, and not to take you for granted. Amen.

5 Renewal of baptismal vows

Then the Bishop says:
You must now declare before God and his Church that you accept the Christian faith into which you were baptized, and in which you will live and grow.
Do you believe and trust in God the Father, who made the world?

Answer   I believe and trust in him.
Do you believe and trust in his Son Jesus Christ, who redeemed mankind?

Answer   I believe and trust in him.

Keyword: 'Redeemed'

Lightbulb

R	E	D	E	E	M	A	L	S
S	T	A	X	D	A	I	H	C
H	I	R	P	C	R	O	S	S
T	D	T	R	A	K	E	D	U
A	S	L	A	V	E	R	Y	S
E	M	I	I	L	T	C	B	E
D	A	P	N	H	U	D	H	J
E	R	J	E	S	C	A	E	A
R	E	D	A	R	T	W	P	R

_____   _____
_____   _____
_____   _____
_____   _____
_____   _____
_____   _____
_____   _____
_____   _____
_____   _____

Connections
Read: Luke 23:26–46
Think: ...about Jesus' death on the cross, and what it cost him to 'redeem' you from slavery to sin.
Pray: Did you really have to die, Jesus? Was there really no other way? Then I'll look at my sin with new eyes, and with new joy receive your forgiveness. Amen.

What I am saying is that as long as the heir is a child, he is no different from a slave, although he owns the whole estate. He is subject to guardians and trustees until the time set by his father. So also, when we were children, we were in slavery under the basic principles of the world. But when the time had fully come, God sent his Son, born of a woman, born under law, to redeem those under law, that we might receive the full rights of sons. Because you are sons, God sent the Spirit of his Son into our hearts, the Spirit who calls out, 'Abba, Father.' So you are no longer a slave, but a son: and since you are a son, God has made you also an heir.

Galatians 4:1–7 (NIV)

Bedrock
1 According to Paul, we can either be a

_____
to sin, or a

_____
of God. Which are you?
2 What do you think are some of the sins that 'enslave' us?
3 What does 'redeem' mean? (v. 5)
4 What did God send to us because we are his 'sons'/'daughters'?

6 Renewal of baptismal vows

Then the Bishop says:
You must now declare before God and his Church that you accept the Christian faith into which you were baptized, and in which you will live and grow.
Do you believe and trust in God the Father, who made the world?

Answer   I believe and trust in him.
Do you believe and trust in his Son Jesus Christ, who redeemed mankind?

Answer   I believe and trust in him.
Do you believe and trust in his Holy Spirit, who gives life to the people of God?

Answer   I believe and trust in him.

Bedrock
1 What does Jesus tell the disciples to do in verse 4?
2 What did Jesus say would happen 'in a few days'?
3 In verse 8, what did Jesus say would happen 'when the Holy Spirit comes on you'?
4 In chapter 2 verse 4, what happened when they were 'filled with the Holy Spirit'?

Connections
Read: Galatians 5:16–25
Think: Which of those spiritual fruits do I need most, today? Write it in the space provided.
Pray: Heavenly Father, by your Spirit within me, please grow in me the spiritual fruit of
that I may live today for your glory. Amen.

Keyword: 'Life'
1 The Holy Spirit is the Spirit of
_____.

2 Who are 'the people of God'?
_____.

3 What does the Holy Spirit give to them? _____.
A definition . . .
The Holy Spirit is (1) _____,
living inside a (2) _____,
giving that person (3)_____.

On one occasion, while he was eating with them, he gave them this command: 'Do not leave Jerusalem, but wait for the gift my Father promised, which you have heard me speak about. For John baptised with water, but in a few days you will be baptised with the Holy Spirit.'
So when they met together, they asked him, 'Lord are you at this time going to restore the kingdom to Israel?'
He said to them: 'It is not for you to know the times or dates the Father has set by his own authority. But you will receive power when the Holy Spirit comes on you: and you will be my witnesses in Jerusalem, and in all Judea and Samaria, and to the ends of the earth.'

The Holy Spirit comes at Pentecost
When the day of Pentecost came they were all together in one place. Suddenly a sound like the blowing of a violent wind came from heaven and filled the whole house where they were sitting. They saw what seemed to be tongues of fire that separated and came to rest on each of them. All of them were filled with the Holy Spirit and began to speak in other tongues as the Spirit enabled them.
Acts 1:4–8; 2:1–4 (NIV)

Lightbulb

I don't want anything to do with the Holy Spirit

I'd like to be 'filled with the Holy Spirit'

0   1   2   3   4   5   6   7   8   9

7 Renewal of baptismal vows

Then the Bishop says:
Do you believe and trust in God the Father, who made the world?

Answer I believe and trust in him.
Do you believe and trust in his Son Jesus Christ, who redeemed mankind?

Answer I believe and trust in him.
Do you believe and trust in his Holy Spirit, who gives life to the people of God?

Answer I believe and trust in him.
The Bishop turns to the congregation and says:
This is the faith of the Church.

All This is **our** faith.
We believe and trust in one God,
Father, Son, and Holy Spirit.

Keyword: 'Our'
1 What is a 'church'?
2 Why doesn't it say '*my* faith'?
3 The Church is more than just (SLIVADDUINI)_____.
This is something we do (HETROGET)_____.

Bedrock
1 What does Paul say the Church is like?
2 What would happen if the whole body was an eye?
3 What would happen if the whole body was an ear?
4 What does Paul's teaching on 'the body' mean for the Church? It means . . .

▷ We're all _____.

▷ We're all _____.

Lightbulb
You could . . .
join a church drama group
visit an elderly person
help in the crèche
read the lesson in church
shop for someone housebound
volunteer to help with the can bank
read to a blind person
cut the grass at church
other . . .

One body, many parts
The body is a unit, though it is made up of many parts; and though all its parts are many, they form one body. So it is with Christ. For we were all baptised by one Spirit into one body—whether Jews or Greeks, slave or free—and we were all given the one Spirit to drink.
Now the body is not made up of one part but of many. If the foot should say, 'Because I am not a hand, I do not belong to the body,' it would not for that reason cease to be part of the body. If the whole body were an eye, where would the sense of hearing be? If the whole body were an ear, where would the sense of smell be? But in fact God has arranged the parts in the body, every one of them, just as he wanted them to be. If they were all one part, where would the body be? As it is, there are many parts, but one body. The eye cannot say to the hand, 'I don't need you!' And the head cannot say to the feet, 'I don't need you!' But God has combined the members of the body and has given greater honour to the parts that lacked it, so that there should be no division in the body, but that its parts should have equal concern for each other. If one part suffers, every part suffers with it; if one part is honoured, every part rejoices with it. Now you are the body of Christ, and each one of you is a part of it.

1 Corinthians 12:12–27 (NIV)

Connections
Read: Matthew 20:1–15
Think: What work might God be calling you to do for him?
Pray: Dear Father, I am young. The whole of my life stretches out before me. Help me to offer my life to you. And give me your strength, that I may serve you. Amen.

8 Renewal of baptismal vows

The candidates stand before the Bishop; he says:

You have come here to be *confirmed*. You stand in the presence of God and his Church. With your own mouth and from your own heart you must declare your allegiance to Christ and your rejection of all that is evil. Therefore I ask these questions:

Do you turn to Christ?

Answer   I turn to Christ.

Do you repent of your sins?

Answer   I repent of my sins.

Do you renounce evil?

Answer

I renounce evil.

Then the Bishop says:

You must now declare before God and his Church that you accept the Christian faith into which you were baptized, and in which you will live and grow.

Do you believe and trust in God the Father, who made the world?

Answer   I believe and trust in him.

Do you believe and trust in his Son Jesus Christ, who redeemed mankind?

Answer   I believe and trust in him.

Do you believe and trust in his Holy Spirit, who gives life to the people of God?

Answer   I believe and trust in him.

The Bishop turns to the congregation and says:

This is the faith of the Church.

All   This is our faith.
We believe and trust in one God,
Father, Son, and Holy Spirit.

Keyword: 'Confirmed'

1 There's some doubt about when you're going to meet a friend. How do you confirm it?

2 Some tickets for a rock concert have been reserved for you until you pay. You've sent the money off. How do you confirm you've got the tickets?

3 You hear a rumour that England have lost to Egypt 2–0. How do you confirm that rumour?

What does 'Confirm' mean?

4 You were baptized as a baby. Someone else made promises for you. How do you confirm those promises?

Bedrock

1 What did Jesus say the bread was like?
2 What happened to the bread?
3 What does that say about Jesus?
4 What did Jesus say the wine was like?
5 What did Jesus tell his followers to do?
6 What does Holy Communion 'do' (v. 26)?

For I received from the Lord what I also passed on to you: The Lord Jesus, on the night he was betrayed, took bread, and when he had given thanks, he broke it and said, 'This is my body, which is for you; do this in remembrance of me.' In the same way, after supper he took the cup, saying, 'This cup is the new covenant in my blood; do this, whenever you drink it, in remembrance of me.' For whenever you eat this bread and drink this cup, you proclaim the Lord's death until he comes.

1 Corinthians 11:23–26 (NIV)

Connections

Take time to look at the week just gone.

Think: In what ways have I hurt those around me? Prepare to confess them in the service.

Have a moment's quiet.

Think: Is there anybody I need to forgive? If so, forgive them, asking God for the strength to do so.

Take time to look ahead to the week to come.

Think: What particularly hard moments do I face? Ask God to equip you for them in the service.

Pray: Thank you, Lord, for these pictures of your love: the broken bread and the wine poured out. Help me to prepare myself properly for Communion, and to meet with you in the service. Amen.